Transforming Congregations

TRANSFORMATIONS
THE EPISCOPAL CHURCH IN THE 21ST CENTURY

Transforming Congregations

JAMES LEMLER

CHURCH PUBLISHING
an imprint of Church Publishing Incorporated, New York

Unless otherwise indicated, all passages from the scriptures are from
the *New Revised Standard Version* of the Bible. © 1989 by the
Division of Christian Education of the National Council of Churches
of Christ in the U.S.A. Used by permission. All rights reserved.

Library of Congress Cataloging-in-Publication Data
Lemler, James B.
    Transforming congregations / by James Lemler.
    p.   cm.
    Includes bibliographical references.
    ISBN 978-0-89869-584-7 (pbk.)
    1. Church renewal. 2. Mission of the church. 3. Episcopal
Church—History—21st century. 4. Christianity—Forecasting.
I. Title.
    BV600.3.L43 2008
    283'.7309051--dc22
                                                    2008000493

Cover design by Stefan Killen Design.
Study guide and interior design by Vicki K. Black.

Printed in the United States of America.

Church Publishing, Incorporated
445 Fifth Avenue
New York, New York 10016
www.churchpublishing.com

        5   4   3   2   1

Contents

a note from the publisher

This series emerged as a partnership between the Office of Mission of the Episcopal Church and Church Publishing, as a contribution to the mission of the church in a new century. We would like to thank James Lemler, series editor, for bringing the initial idea to us and for facilitating the series. We also want to express our gratitude to the Office of Mission for two partnership grants: the first brought all the series authors together for two creative days of brainstorming and fellowship; and the second is helping to further publicize the books of the series to the clergy and lay people of the Episcopal Church.

Series Preface

B e ye transformed" (KJV). "Be transformed by the renewing of your minds" (NRSV). "Fix your attention on God. You'll be changed from the inside out" (*The Message*). Thus St. Paul exhorted the earliest Christian community in his writing to the Romans two millennia ago. This exhortation was important for the early church and it is urgent for the Episcopal Church to heed as it enters the twenty-first century. Be transformed. Be changed from the inside out.

Perhaps no term fits the work and circumstances of the church in the twenty-first century better than "transformation." We are increasingly aware of the need for change as we become ever more mission-focused in the life of the church, both internationally and domestically. But society as a whole is rapidly moving in new directions, and mission cannot be embraced in an unexamined way, relying on old cultural and ecclesiastical stereotypes and assumptions.

This new series, *Transformations: The Episcopal Church in the 21st Century,* addresses these issues in realistic and hopeful ways. Each book focuses on one area within the Episcopal Church that is urgently in need of transformation in order for the church to be effective in the twenty-first century: vocation, evangelism, preaching, congregational life, getting to know the Bible, leadership, Christian formation, worship, and stewardship. Each volume explains why a changed vision is essential, gives robust theological and biblical foundations, offers guidelines to best practices and positive trends, describes the necessary tools for change, and imagines how transformation will look.

In this volume I will take on the topic of congregations and mission, drawing on my experience as a parish priest, seminary dean, and director of mission for the Episcopal Church. Local communities of faith are the frontline of mission. It is essential, therefore, for congregations to experience enhanced congregational mission and utilize tools for vitality, strength, and health. How can our patterns of congregational life and mission adjust to changing culture without abandoning what Episcopalians stand for? How can local faith communities stay resilient and hopeful? What styles and practices of spirituality do most to enrich our mission? I will provide a variety of models to feed our growing hunger to move forward in mission and hope to a more abundant future.

Like Christians in the early church, today we live in a secular culture that can be apathetic and even hostile to Christianity. Living in a setting where people are not familiar with the message or narrative of Christian believing requires new responses and new kinds of mission for the Body of Christ. We believe this is a hopeful time for spiritual seekers and inquirers in the church. The gospel itself is fresh for this century. God's love is vibrant and real; God's mission can transform people's hopes and lives. Will we participate in the transformation? Will we be bearers and agents of transformation for others? Will we ourselves be transformed? This is the call and these are the urgent questions for the Episcopal Church in the twenty-first century.

But first, seek to be transformed. Fix your attention on God. You'll be changed from the inside out.

JAMES B. LEMLER, *series editor*

Acknowledgments

What a privilege it is to serve, experience, assist, and form congregations. I am committed to congregations and do believe that they are the frontline of mission. Thus I am honored to offer this resource for the theological reflection and practical development of local communities of faith and hope that leaders will find it useful. This writing reflects over thirty years of service to them as a clergyperson, leadership developer, and consultant. Again... what a privilege!

Congregations are communities of thanksgiving. They gather to thank God for the gifts of God's love and redemption. They express their thanksgiving through service and compassion to the wider world, and they have much for which they can be thankful. It is appropriate that a book on congregations begins with the offering of thanks by its author. I offer thanks for:

> ✦ The local communities of faith that I have served as a priest and leader: St. James Cathedral, South Bend; Christ Church Cathedral, Indianapolis; the DePauw University Chapel; Trinity Episcopal Church, Indianapolis; Seabury-Western Theological Seminary, Evanston; Christ Church, Greenwich; and St. Luke's and St. Matthew's Churches, Evanston and

St. Michael's Church, New York City, in which I have served as honorary assisting priest.

◆ The congregations, dioceses, and institutions where I have had the opportunity to teach about congregational leadership and vitality, as well as the congregations that have offered stories and learning for me, much of which is reflected in this book. (All the congregational narratives found here are true, but the names of congregations are fictional since true congregational case studies would require much more than the short vignettes possible in this writing.)

◆ The wonderful colleagues in mission and ministry in all of the settings where I have served, especially wardens and vestries, pastoral assistants and colleagues, and fellow teachers and consultants in leadership and congregational development. I particularly want to thank the two Presiding Bishops whom I have served, the Most Reverend Frank T. Griswold III and the Most Reverend Katharine Jefferts Schori, for their support, vision, and leadership.

◆ The community of learning about congregational development and leadership, particularly the Lilly Endowment, Inc.; the Alban Institute; the Center for Congregations; the Seabury Institute; the Church Pension Fund research department; and the Congregational Development, Research, and Mission Leadership units of the Episcopal Church Center.

◆ Colleagues who are authors in the *Transformations* series, many of whom are long-time friends and associates and others who are new colleagues, all with the same goal of providing useful resources for local communities of faith and their leadership. Thanks also to editors Cynthia Shattuck and Vicki Black for their unflagging efforts and to the two organizations that make such resources possible, Church Publishing Incorporated and its parent, the Church Pension Fund.

Finally, I want to offer thanks for the foundational family relationship that has offered support, strength, and love for my journey in life, faith, and ministry. Sharon, my wife of thirty plus years is truly one of the wisest, most creative and caring human beings I know. Our three daughters, Kate, Anna, and Maria, are continuing sources of joy and honest observers about life, belief, and communities of faith.

I am deeply thankful for all of these people, communities, and gifts. God is in the midst of them, and through them God has shaped me for this offering and other forms of service. There is an ascription of praise written by St. Paul that is included in the office of Morning Prayer. I have prayed it with congregations and their leaders for three decades, not only in daily prayer but at meetings, retreats, and conference. It is the reflection of my experience of God's purpose and presence, and it is a summary of the hope of this writing and series of books.

Glory to God whose power, working in us, can do infinitely more than we can ask or imagine: Glory to God from generation to generation in the Church, and in Christ Jesus for ever and ever.

And I respond with so many others: "Amen."

Shall We Gather
at the River?

I have to make a confession at the very start: I love congregations. I find them endlessly fascinating and continually
significant. Being in them, leading them, learning about
them, consulting with them—all have been at the center of
my life and ministry. Congregations are communities in
which people are transformed in their faith and life. The
Spirit of God is at work in them—in their rich histories,
present mission dynamics, and future possibilities for
service. God is in their midst. Congregations are at the heart
and center of the mission of God's church.

There are over three hundred thousand local communities of faith in the United States, approximately seventy-
four hundred of them congregations of the Episcopal
Church. These faith communities are found in every sort
of setting, and each one is unique in its identity. People
engage God and the practices of Christian faith in ongoing
and significant ways within their congregations. These
local communities of faith generate profound and imagina-
tive mission both here and around the world. Yet congregations are also complex entities. They can experience

vitality, strength, and growth. Conversely, they can experience challenge, weakness, and decline. Congregations require leadership, clarity of purpose, and vision for the future. Their life cannot be left unexamined and their present and future require strategy and action.

This book is written for congregations—their members and their leaders—and for people who care about congregations and their effective mission. It includes an assessment of congregational life and a theological reflection for congregational mission and transformation. It describes the characteristics and attributes of strong and vital congregations, and offers up spiritual practices that enhance the lives of individual believers and congregations themselves.

This book also recognizes that congregations cannot be transformed apart from their sense of mission, which is an even more essential focus, topic, and reality for the church at this time. By "mission" I mean the primary purpose, work, and call of God and of the church. God's mission is the continuing purpose of God in redeeming and restoring all humanity and, indeed, the whole universe. The church's mission is the manifestation of God's mission in a particular time, place, and context. Local congregations reflect God's mission, and they live out this broader mission in their own settings with their own identity, values, and priorities.

we begin with water

To engage the mission of God's church, we begin with congregations in their mission. To reflect on their character and mission, we begin with water. We dive into the powerful waters of baptism which flow in and through local congregations. We negotiate the fast-moving waters of change that are all around us in our contemporary context and world. Here begins my story of congregational life and mission, in the waters of God's grace and love.

I served one particular congregation for many years and learned a great deal about God and gospel in that community of faith as we prayed, proclaimed, served, learned, and reached out together. There are many stories to be told, but one is especially appropriate in thinking about the life, mission, and identity of that congregation.

It is the story of worship on a glorious Sunday morning. The morning was bright and beautiful, but its brightness and beauty came from something more than the sun in the sky and the lush autumn day. It was the brightness of Christian faith and hope and the beauty of God's people gathered for prayer and proclamation.

This was a celebration of Holy Baptism, and what a celebration it was. Children, adults, black, white, offspring of long-time church members as well as people for whom church life was a new experience gathered to be showered with God's abundant grace and love, to be renewed and transformed in life, to be gifted with the powerful, playful Spirit of God, and to be enrolled in the expression of faith in which God would be joined to them in this life and in the life to come. There was not a great deal of water, but there was enough . . . a sufficiency of water to flow with the purpose and power of God. There was enough water to transform and change their lives forever.

This congregation was answering the question raised in a beloved African American spiritual, "Shall we gather at the river?" We sang this song in procession to the font that morning. More importantly, we answered the question raised in the singing, "Yes, we'll gather at the river, the beautiful, the beautiful river. . . ." We were affirming and affirmative about what God was doing in the waters of baptism as we gathered at the beautiful river of God's love and grace.

Christian congregations gather at the river frequently and do this baptismal action regularly. They welcome people into the household of God and, in so doing, they proclaim the identity of Christian people individually and corporately. Individuals are "marked as Christ's own forever." They belong to Christ and are enfolded in Christ's love. They are made citizens of God's kingdom and members of God's church. Their identity is one that includes generosity, proclamation, service, forgiveness, compassion, justice, and respect.

The same is true for the community of faith. Its identity is also shaped and proclaimed in the action of Holy Baptism. Through this action, the Christian community is identified as a community of proclamation, service, and reconciliation. It is a community of invitation and hospitality at its very core. Thus, it is a community of mission. We can actually see the mission of the church as we look into the waters of baptism. And we can see that we are to be a church of mission, a church of purpose, a church that lives out its baptismal identity day by day.

"We thank you, Father, for the waters of Baptism. In it we are buried with Christ in his death. By it we share in his resurrection. Through it we are reborn by the Holy Spirit" (BCP 306). What powerful waters they are! What a river of grace it is. "Shall we gather at the river?" It is a question for people of faith and their congregations. Congregations exist to be baptismal communities gathered around God's word and purpose. They are empowered by God's Spirit to embody and engage God's mission in the world. The waters of grace continue to flow.

the waters of scripture

God has used waters to express purpose, mission, love, and grace since the beginning. Literally "in the beginning" a significant part of God's creation was water, the primeval great waters out of which other forms of life came. "In the beginning when God created the heavens and the earth, the earth was a formless void and darkness covered the face of the deep, while a wind from God swept over the face of the waters" (Genesis 1:1–2). The watery creation progresses: "And God said, 'Let there be a dome in the midst of the waters, and let it separate the waters from the waters'" (Genesis 1:6).

The Hebrew scriptures continue to tell stories of powerful and transforming waters. The whole earth is transformed, as the Genesis narrative tells the story of Noah and the great flood. Everything is changed for a new beginning, a beginning that can happen only in God's purpose and will. God said, "I will send rain on the earth for forty days and forty nights." And when the flood waters indeed began to flow on the earth, "Noah with his sons and his wife and his sons' wives went into the ark to escape the waters of the flood" (Genesis 7:4, 7). However, the story does not end with the primeval flood, but with a promise and a purpose. After "the waters were dried up from the earth" (Genesis 8:7), God clearly speaks the promise:

> As for me, I am establishing my covenant with you and your descendants after you, and with every living creature that is with you.... This is the sign of the covenant that I make between me and you and every living creature that is with you, for all future generations: I have set my bow in the clouds, and it shall be a sign of the covenant between me and the earth. (Genesis 9:9–10, 12–13)

The watery story keeps flowing in the events of the Exodus. God's purpose—the redemption of God's people—happens in and through water. The waters of the mighty Red Sea are divided so that God's people may pass over from slavery to freedom, from oppression to redemption, from hopelessness to new possibility. God gives Moses a poignant command so that deep waters lead to life rather than death

> Then the LORD said to Moses, "Why do you cry out to me? Tell the Israelites to go forward. But you lift up your staff, and stretch out your hand over the sea and divide it, that the Israelites may go into the sea on dry ground." (Exodus 14:15–16)

Waters are powerful as the Hebrew scriptures continue to tell the story, even as they flow from God's own temple and throne as envisioned by the prophet Ezekiel. At the entrance of the temple the prophet is shown water "flowing from below the threshold of the temple toward the east" and "from below the south end of the threshold of the temple, south of the altar." Ezekiel is led through the waters—ankle-deep, then knee-deep and up to the waist, and finally deep enough to swim in. He is told, "Wherever the river goes, every living creature that swarms will live" (Ezekiel 47:1, 9). In this river the prophet sees the image of God's flowing grace, love, and purpose.

Here we have a vision of God's mission as reflected in the waters of creation, redemption, and restoration:

✦ *God creates.* God brings creative power and purpose to chaos. God creates life and extends that life throughout the universe, to human beings, and in the face of death itself. God also creates a community, the people Israel, to serve and live out God's mission in the world.

✦ *God redeems.* God saves God's people from slavery and oppression in Egypt, leading them through the waters of redemption to new life and hope. This is the primary action of God's mission, redeeming God's people. The prophets proclaim redemption for

God's people even when they have sinned, and some of the prophets name the universal redemption which God will give to all people.

♦ *God restores*. A central part of God's mission is the action of restoration. God restores that which is broken. God searches for the lost and renews the spirits of God's people when they are flagging. God empowers return for exiles and the restoration of Jerusalem itself.

Nor does the story of God's mission through water end with the Hebrew scriptures; it continues on a river bank in the Gospel of Mark. Jesus of Nazareth goes to his cousin John the baptizer for a ceremonial washing, but something more happens in the Jordan River. Jesus' identity is proclaimed in divine voice and action. "You are my Son, the Beloved," a voice from heaven announces, and a dove descends on Jesus as a visible sign of the Spirit of God at work (Mark 1:10–11).

Jesus takes his identity seriously. He lives as God's beloved child, announcing God's kingdom, healing, preaching, inviting, serving, and caring. He uses water to describe his mission. "I will give you living water," Jesus tells a Samaritan woman at a well. She was skeptical, but he told her more. "You will never thirst again. I will quench your thirst forever" (John 4). Jesus' mission involves creation, redemption, and restoration.

♦ *Jesus creates*. Jesus creates hope and new beginnings for people as he proclaims the in-breaking sovereignty of God. He gives the gift of life to people and even raises some from the dead.

♦ *Jesus redeems*. Jesus' primary action of mission is redemption. He redeems human beings who are alienated and broken through his actions of healing and welcome. His primary action of mission and redemption is his cross and resurrection.

♦ *Jesus restores.* The mission of Jesus is one of restoration, breaking down walls of hostility and enmity so that a new and restored humanity might be made. He constantly invites the outcast into the loving embrace of God.

This was Jesus' mission, and he entrusted that mission to his followers, creating a community of mission through discipleship and service. The waters of baptism are the sign and symbol of that mission and community. Jesus' disciples carried on the mission and continued to use water as a sign of the mission of individual believers and the community. The New Testament epistles include a continual call to the recollection of baptismal and missional identity on the part of local communities of faith.

In a similar way, the early Christian writers spoke and preached often on the meaning of the waters of grace. They focused on the power of the baptismal relationship and identity. Cyprian, who was Bishop of Carthage in the third century, described his discovery of the love and power of God within the waters of baptism in his own life in this way:

> I was myself so entangled and constrained by the very many errors of my former life that I could not believe it possible for me to escape from them. . . . But when the stain of my earlier life had been washed away by the help of the water of baptism . . . and I had been restored such as to make me a new human being . . . what before had seemed difficult was now easy.[1]

The waters of mission and transformation continue to flow. We are inheritors of these waters of grace, life, and spirit that shape our identity and transform us in their power. We live in them, and we "live" them. The church became ever more focused on these waters in the latter half of the twentieth century, and this focus continues into the twenty-first century as we have become ever more aware of the power of Holy Baptism to bring about the transformation we seek.

baptismal theology

A baptismal revolution began in the life of the church about fifty years ago. We see the effect of that revolution in many different aspects of the Episcopal Church: the baptism-centered theology of the 1979 Book of Common Prayer; the entry of women to ordained ministry; the recognition of the role and leadership of the laity; the admission of infants and children to Holy Communion; new approaches to Christian formation of children, young people, and adults; new modes of raising up and training ordained and lay leaders; and the acknowledged priority of local congregations as the focus of mission for the church. Thus baptismal theology provides a vital starting point for theological reflection in the church today.

At its core, baptismal theology is a theology of transformation and mission, emphasizing both the change that occurs in the life of individual believers and the meaning of mission for the church. Baptismal theology has moved the starting point of theology about the church. The theology of the church no longer begins "from above"— that is, from a hierarchical perspective of the church as it was organized for the fifteen hundred years of Christendom. Rather, it begins "from below," or I would prefer to say "from the waters"—that is, from local communities of faith where the people of God gather for mission and ministry. The authority of mission comes from the whole people of God practicing their faith in local congregations and daily life, rather than from hierarchical structures.

This baptismal theology has transformed the Episcopal Church in the United States of America, as well as in other parts of the Anglican Communion and in churches of various traditions. It has been taken particularly seriously in the Episcopal Church because of our tradition of democratic polity and lay empowerment and because of the greater congregational focus of American religion. It is not entirely understood, however, in those parts of the Anglican Communion that tend to manifest a model of polity and authority that depend on greater hierarchical authority.

The Baptismal Covenant, as articulated so clearly and powerfully in the Book of Common Prayer of the Episcopal Church, is illustrative of this church's baptismal theology. This covenant reflects a baptismal theology of service, openness, and transformation, and expresses a sense of empowerment, respect, and inclusion. This baptismal theology has transformed the congregations of the Episcopal Church themselves. Local communities of faith realize that they are at the core of mission and ministry and are seeking new ways of partnership with diocesan and national church structures of mission. Leadership is perceived as partnership between laity and clergy with both sets of believers to be necessary for furthering mission. Baptismal theology has created an environment of welcome, hospitality, and invitation in local congregations. It has changed congregations through these mechanisms:

> ◆ *The public celebration of baptism.* Public baptism has become the norm in Episcopal congregational life, giving people the regular opportunity to engage this ritual experience of identity and transformation.

* *Baptismal education.* Congregations utilize several means of baptismal education. Some occur prior to baptism for adults or for parents of infants and small children, while others focus on the renewal of baptismal vows and reaffirmation formation for youth and adults.

* *Baptismal theology and spiritual renewal events.* New resources have been developed for learning about baptism in children and adult formation and retreat settings. There are also retreat materials focusing on the meaning of baptism.

Baptismal theology is at its heart a theology of identity, reflecting the core identity of believers and communities of faith. We often ask, "What is the church to *do*?" But the prior, more important question is, "What is the church to *be*?" We are to be a community of faith in the midst of change, and we are to be a community of faith leading change. We are to be a community where people discover that they can depend on God and be enfolded in the love of God even in the midst of such rapid change and transition in their own lives. We are to be a community where people can experience and call upon the sustaining gifts of the Holy Baptism.

The prayer from the baptismal service describes the hope and joy which belong to the believer:

> Heavenly Father, we thank you that by water and the Holy Spirit you have bestowed upon these your servants the forgiveness of sin, and have raised them to the new life of grace. Sustain them, O Lord, in your Holy Spirit. Give them an inquiring and discerning heart, the courage to will and to persevere, a spirit to know and to love you, and the gift of joy and wonder in all your works. (BCP 308)

In the midst of change, we can find hope. In the midst of transition, we can find joy. In the midst of uncertainty, we can find Christ. We are a community called to lead change. Our mission is one of transformation, of transforming the world. The Baptismal Covenant describes our call to transformation with clarity.

✦ We are called to trust God as our Creator, Redeemer, and Sanctifier.

The foundational questions that introduce the Baptismal Covenant in the Book of Common Prayer are about belief and trust. Will we believe and trust in the God who creates, redeems, and sanctifies human beings, the God who is present and active in the world and in our own lives? *Trusting belief* and *believing trust* are at the basis of life in faith and relationship with God.

✦ We are called to continue in the apostles' teaching and fellowship, in the breaking of bread, and in the prayers.

Learning and *worship* are transformative. Congregations are communities where people gather to learn about faith, tradition, and God's work in the world. Learning for all ages is one of the marks of vital congregational life as this learning changes people in serious and hopeful ways. Worship is directly connected to learning as a source of transformation for people. The human spirit is changed and enlivened through practices of prayer and worship.

✦ We are called to persevere in resisting evil, and, whenever we fall into sin, to repent and return to the Lord.

Christian congregations are moral communities by their very nature. They offer a setting of moral transformation, helping people to find a moral compass in their own living. Congregations are also communities that actually help to change the world. They are communities of *forgiveness* and *reconciliation* in a culture where there is much isolation and fragmentation.

✦ We are called to proclaim by word and example the Good News of God in Christ.

Congregations change people through the practices of *evangelism.* They invite people to a new experience and vision of life. They proclaim a message of hope, life, and compassion through their words and their actions. The work of evangelism does not end with the arrival of people within the local community of faith. Rather, the message is continually proclaimed, and human beings are invited more deeply into relationship with God through their incorporation, learning, and eventual sending.

✦ We are called to seek and serve Christ in all persons, loving our neighbor as ourselves.

We know it in local congregations and in the larger church as well. *Service* transforms people and the world. Positive change is wrought through a congregation's commitment to feed the hungry, visit the prisoner, care for the sick and the lonely, and provide shelter for the homeless. Both those who serve and those who are served are changed through the expressions of service and compassion. The embrace of the United Nations' eight Millennium Development Goals throughout the church and its congregations is contributing to positive change on a global basis.

✦ We are called to strive for justice and peace among all people, and to respect the dignity of every human being.

People are changed when they act justly and make peace, and, in turn, they help to change the world into a reflection of the love and kingdom of God. Local congregations gather believers to learn about and practice *justice, peace, and respect.* In that setting, people become internally changed through these gospel commitments. Their own souls are refreshed, and they represent these dynamics of God's purpose and sovereignty on this earth.

Human beings are transformed and changed by these baptismal promises. Will we proclaim the gospel and invite people into the community of faith? Will we be changed through learning, prayer, and service? Will we change the world through respect, reconciliation, and love? These questions reflect our most basic identity and purpose as the Christian church. The congregation itself is a place of change and transformation for people. It is part of the purpose of the local community of faith to offer modes and experiences of transformation. Local communities of faith (congregations, chaplaincies, and other local expressions of worship and service) are by their very nature communities where people seek and experience transformation through prayer, service, fellowship, and formation.

a new theology of mission

Closely intertwined with the renewal of a baptismal theology in the church of the late twentieth and early twenty-first centuries has been the emergence of a transformed theology of mission. This theology describes the purpose, call, and action of the church in a forceful and significant way. There have been several contributors to this emerging theology. One of the most influential was David Bosch, a South African theologian of mission who died tragically in an automobile accident at a young age. His contribution was to analyze scripture, tradition, and the present moment of the church's life from the perspective of mission. How has the church moved forward in its call to teach, invite, heal, reconcile, restore, and transform? How does Holy Scripture speak of mission; how is mission perceived as the primary work of God and of God's church?

Bosch's book is appropriately entitled *Transforming Mission*. He identifies momentous paradigm shifts that have occurred in the church's context and in the church itself, shifts that have urged the church of the twenty-first century to become much more "missional," much more focused on mission. The title of the book itself has a double meaning: "Transforming mission means both that mission is to be understood as an activity that transforms reality and that there is a constant need for mission itself to be transformed."[2] Bosch offers a description that is applicable for global mission and for the domestic mission of congregations, dioceses, and a national expression of the church. He clearly perceives mission as transformation, the action that transforms reality and human life.

Bosch's reflections join with those of others throughout the world as mission becomes a central focus for theology in our own day. It has also become a focus for the theological reflection and action plan depicted in the work of the Episcopal Church's Standing Commission on World Mission through the publication of its report entitled "Companions in Transformation." This work clearly perceives world mission as companionship involving and leading to transformation. "Companions in Transformation" describes the power of God's mission made real in the mission of the church in this way:

> As we meet Christ in our neighbor, God's mission transforms both the world and community of Jesus as it rediscovers its call to discipleship. As a missionary church witnesses in word and deed,

God works through it to reconcile all peoples in Christ and renew the face of the earth.[3]

This global theology of mission has had a great impact on the practice of worldwide mission within the Episcopal Church. The number of companion relationships between Episcopal Church dioceses and congregations and those overseas continues to grow. The financial investment in global mission is one of the single greatest parts of the annual budget of the Episcopal Church. People are experiencing transformation by offering their own lives for a period of time as missionaries, Volunteers for Mission, and members of the Young Adult Service Corps. New ventures in global mission and world mission educational opportunities for congregations are expanding all the time.

The theology of mission comes even closer to home. Many theologians of mission have been asking theological and practical questions about mission in North America, calling the church to recognize that this part of God's world is indeed a field of mission and calling the church to change, if it is to be effective in this field. The premise is that the church in North America must be transformed into a church with a primary awareness of being sent for mission. Darrell Guder, one of the most articulate North American mission theologians, describes the call and the opportunity in this way:

> Two things have become quite clear to those who care about the church and its mission. On the one hand, the churches of North America have been dislocated from their prior social role of chaplain to the culture and society and have lost their once privileged positions of influence. Religious life in general and the churches in particular have increasingly been relegated to the private spheres of life. The churches have a great opportunity in these

circumstances, however. The same pressures that threaten the continued survival of some churches, disturb the confidence of others, and devalue the meaning of them all can actually be helpful in providing an opening for new possibilities. Emerging into view on the far side of the church's long experience of Christendom is a wide vista of potential for the people of God in the post-modern and post-Christian world of North America. The present is a wildly opportune moment for churches to find themselves and to put on the garments of their calling, their vocation.[4]

The Episcopal Church, like most mainline denominations, has experienced the cultural pressures and sense of marginalization Guder describes. We have seen the impact of these changes in our membership: there has been a gradual but real numerical decline in Episcopal congregations for several decades now. There are many reasons for this lack of growth:

♦ We work under a former assumption that the culture is Christian and will yield people to us who are ready to be "Episcopalian-ized."

♦ We are too much a church of the predominant middle class and white culture, not welcoming new and traditionally underserved groups within our society (although this is beginning to change, with growing Asian, African, West Indian, and Latino congregations).

♦ We have not recruited or retained younger generations, especially young adults.

♦ Our birth rate (like that of other mainline denominations) continues to decline. We cannot replace ourselves any longer.

♦ We say that we want to grow, but in many of our congregations we are not ready to embrace the change necessary for growth.

However, the primary reason for our decline is that we have not envisioned and become engaged in ministries of evangelism, invitation, and hospitality in our congregations in ways that meet the present rapidly changing world around us. Some commentators suggest that our present numerical decline is due to moral and ethical changes in the church, but that is not the case. We have not grown because we have not set our sights on invitation and incorporation in this new century. It is urgent that we do so, that we embrace the mission of evangelism and welcome, and that we plan for it in our local congregations.

This is a time for a dramatically new vision. The current predicament of churches in North America requires more than a mere tinkering with long-assumed notions about the identity and mission of the church. Instead, as many knowledgeable observers have noted, there is a need for reinventing or rediscovering the church in this new kind of world. — *Darrell Guder*

This urgent moment for the church is also a hopeful one. New forms of mission and evangelism are presenting themselves in communities of faith today, and some congregations are beginning to establish plans and strategies for evangelism. Even more hopeful are the identity and nature of the Episcopal Church itself. We are a church of openness, spiritual vitality, and mutual respect. Much of our identity connects well with the postmodern world and culture in which we find ourselves. We are a church which does not take a judgmental stance regarding people or their lives. Our polity is one that involves lay people at every level of decision-making. We possess genuine respect for inquiry and do not demand that people adhere to certain strict doctrinal and dogmatic tenets for participation. We value our rich tradition of spirituality and encourage a variety of spiritual approaches and styles. We are a church for the moment in so many ways.

However, we simply must change. We must become much more intentional in our focus on proclamation and invitation. We cannot be satisfied with the way we were, the time-worn customs of worship and community life. They have allowed us to turn in on ourselves and to have patterns of community of life that are unintentionally closed to newcomers. Our worship must change. Our modes of communication, advertising, and welcome must change. Certainly, we have the capacity to do all of these things, if we want to do them.

Congregations that are alive are congregations that can embrace change, help people in the midst of changes of their lives, and offer experiences of transformation. To change is not an option in the mission of transformation that belongs to the church. It is not an option; it is the character and nature of local communities of faith in the twenty-first century.

mission in the twenty-first century

Like many churches in North America today, the Episcopal Church is in a process of defining its own missional identity and work, of putting on "the garments" of our baptismal vocation. One of the most effective champions of a mission-based approach for diocesan and congregational life is Claude Payne, the retired Bishop of Texas. Working with other leaders, Payne changed the focus of the Diocese of Texas to mission and hosted national conferences during his episcopate entitled "A Clear Vision." That is precisely what he brought to his diocese and its congregations. Making the distinction between "mission" and "maintenance" (terms that originated with pastoral theologian Howard Hanchey), Bishop Payne joined with lay colleague Hamilton Beazley to envision a mission-focused church for the twenty-first century. Like Darrell Guder, they believe the church today "has a wondrous opportunity before it: to once again proclaim the Word of God to the world." At the same time, they believe this opportunity for mission is a matter of utmost importance:

> If the Christian community can recover its sense of being God's agent for transformation, and if it can recover its passion for making disciples, it can reach out to the spiritually hungry and offer them the rich banquet of the Christian life. The spiritual hunger in America, like any other kind of hunger, will be satisfied one way or another, or the hungry will die.[5]

THE 2020 VISION

An approach similar to Bishop Payne's was taken by the Standing Commission on Domestic Mission and Evangelism following its inception in 1998. As the chair of that commission, I was able to work with a diverse group of church leaders to consider the mission, theology, needs, and potential of the Episcopal Church, especially through its congregations. The result was a vision for mission awareness and action at every level and manifestation of the church's work.

Christened the "2020 Vision," this work framed a focus and initial strategy for effective domestic mission on the cusp of the twenty-first century. The vision named ingredients for effective evangelism and congregational growth and vitality, including five elements for its implementation and effectiveness.

1. Creative strategies of evangelism.

2. Prayer and spiritual development.

3. Recruiting and equipping innovative leaders.

4. Strengthening congregational life.

5. Focusing on children, youth, and campus ministries.

These elements provide a cohesive fabric for the vitality and growth of the church. They apply equally to each congregation and to larger expressions of the church, at the diocesan, national, and Communion-wide levels.

> Called to restore all people to unity with God and each other in Christ. . . . We commit to being a healthy, dynamic, inviting church, reflective of the diversity of our society, deeply rooted in faith and the gospel, so that we live out our baptismal promise to be disciples who make disciples of Jesus Christ. — *the 2020 Vision*

Each of five elements focuses on a necessary area of mission and progress in mission, and together they offer important possibilities and questions for transformation.

1. Creative strategies of evangelism.

The primary question here is this. Will the church develop intentional, creative, and committed plans and actions for evangelism? Too often these plans and actions have been absent in the church and its congregations. The 2020 Vision has raised the bar for all of us, maintaining that clear and active evangelism is utterly necessary for the church to thrive. This has had a great effect on the priorities of the larger Episcopal Church.

2. Prayer and spiritual development.

This is an age of spiritual awareness and practices. A church that is transformed and transforming must have a strong spiritual foundation. Spiritual wisdom informs decision-making. The congregation itself is a place of spiritual transformation where people are drawn closer in their relationship with God. Wider manifestations of the church (the larger Episcopal Church and dioceses) have the responsibility of providing resources for spiritual experience and transformation. Local congregations shape their lives and programs for spiritual empowerment and enrichment.

3. Recruiting and equipping innovative leaders.

Mission depends to a very great extent on leaders and leadership. A transformed church requires transformed leaders. This element of the 2020 Vision calls on the church to recruit and develop leaders that are innovative, entrepreneurial, and evangelical. It envisions leadership education at all levels of the church.

4. Strengthening congregational life.

The recognition that congregations are at the center and forefront of mission requires intentional forms of development and capacity building for local communities of faith. The good news is that many such resources exist, and this element calls on the larger church and dioceses to develop further resources to support congregational development. It also calls every congregation to prepare a plan for its development.

5. Focusing on children, youth, and college ministries.

A healthy, thriving, vital, and dynamic church must focus on its younger generations. This is a call for new types of ministries for children, youth, and young adults in the whole Episcopal Church and its congregations. The only way the church will counter its underrepresentation in these age groups is by focusing on them and their needs.

The importance of these elements of the 2020 Vision was sometimes overlooked as some Episcopalians expressed more concern about the part of the vision emphasizing doubling the size of the Episcopal Church. That was unfortunate, because the elements themselves are the heart of the 2020 Vision and are directly pertinent to the mission of the Episcopal Church in its national, diocesan, and congregational manifestations.

THE NATIONAL CHURCH

Mission theology and focus permeate the work of the Episcopal Church as a national and international organization. Presiding Bishop Frank Griswold and his staff, in concert with the General Convention and the Executive Council, sought to develop an intentional design and strategy to organize the Episcopal Church Center and its work around the theology and practice of mission, and this mission focus and framework now continuously shape the work of the wider Episcopal Church. At the Episcopal Church Center, several questions are regularly asked regarding program and work:

♦ Does this particular action further the mission of restoration, renewal, and reconciliation?

♦ Does it enhance the mission in partnership with other levels and manifestations of church life (international, provincial, diocesan, and congregational)?

♦ Are people passionate about it, and does it portray the gospel in vigorous ways?

The 2006 General Convention of the Episcopal Church gave ample evidence of the enthusiasm with which we are responding to these questions. The mission energy of the convention was palpable in these and several other ways:

✦ *A clear embrace of the Millennium Development Goals.* A grassroots mission exhilaration showed itself in the focus on how the church does its ministry of service and compassion through the vehicle of the Millennium Development Goals and their commitment to eradicate global poverty and hopelessness.[6]

✦ *Our response to the ongoing post-Katrina experience and tragedy.* Efforts to make a real difference in housing and religious leadership were developed.

✦ *A mission funding initiative.* The decision was made to begin working toward the development of major funds for the mission of the Episcopal Church.

✦ *A renewed commitment to evangelism.* New vision and energy for evangelism and the planting of new congregations was evident.

✦ *An emphasis on ministries of compassion.* New work to combat domestic poverty was envisioned.

✦ *The election of the 26th Presiding Bishop.* The mission focus was an important part of the Spirit's work in the election of Bishop Katharine Jefferts Schori.

The new Presiding Bishop began her ministry by focusing on mission. In her investiture sermon, Bishop Jefferts Schori made it clear that her top priority would be God's mission and its activities. Her initial work of leadership in the Episcopal Church has involved building the networks and organizing the activities for mission in the coming decade.

MISSION PRIORITIES

The Episcopal Church's governance and budgeting process reflect mission awareness and focus as well. Two recent reports—"Moving Ahead in Mission" and

"Mission and Resources"—provide narratives regarding the financial resources of the Episcopal Church, looking at both income and expenses and how these resources are used for mission. These reports are organized around the mission priorities established by the church's General Convention in 2003 and modified with a few significant modifications in the 2006 Convention. The mission priorities begin with an engaging preface:

> We offer these mission priorities as an expression of our commitment to Jesus Christ. We are committed to the importance of our ministry of reconciliation and communion at every level of our communion. We embrace diversity and seek to promote inclusion and power sharing which underlie and inform all priorities, decisions, and all that we do. In faithfulness to these commitments, we continue to honor our covenants and partnerships with domestic and overseas dioceses. We recognize that the work of mission depends in large part on increasing the leadership capacity of clergy and lay leaders of the church.

The mission priorities then follow:

> 1. *Justice and peace:* Promoting justice and peace for all of God's creation and continuing and accelerating the leadership role and programs of the Episcopal Church, which support the eight (8) Millennium Development Goals in the dioceses of the Episcopal Church and in the world.

> 2. *Young adults, youth and children:* Reaching out to young adults, youth, and children through intentional inclusion and full incorporation in the thinking, work, worship, and structure of the church.

> 3. *Reconciliation and evangelism:* Reconciling and engaging those who do not know Christ by partici-

pating in God's mission of reconciling all things to Christ and proclaiming the gospel to those who are not yet members of the church.

4. *Congregational transformation:* Revitalizing and transforming congregations through commitment to leadership development, spiritual growth, lifelong learning, dynamic and inclusive worship, greater diversity, and mission.

5. *Partnerships:* Reaffirming the importance of our partnerships with provinces of the Anglican Communion and beyond and our relationships with ecumenical and interfaith partners.

The priorities themselves stem from the mission theology and practices that are shaping the Episcopal Church today. They recognize the importance of mission in domestic arenas of justice, peace, ministry with the next generations, evangelism, and congregational vitality. They possess a strong global focus as well with their emphasis on partnerships and commitment to the Millennium Development Goals. Local congregations are increasingly embracing and engaging these mission priorities in their mission of education, congregational development, and service.

mission in congregations

The theology of mission comes even closer to home when it affects the local community of faith and its beliefs and practices. Congregations are becoming more aware of the mission foundation and theology of their work, as we now understand that *effective congregations in the twenty-first century will be those that have a clear mission focus and purpose.* They will be many different sizes, in a variety of locations, and reflect a range of styles. Their commonality will be mission awareness, focus, and implementation. The characteristics of such a mission-generated and mission-focused congregation are becoming more apparent to us at the present moment, and include:

- *Clarity of mission.* A congregation needs to know who it is and what it is called to accomplish.

- *Open communication.* Good information flow in the congregation is essential, with dialogue that is truthful, direct, and kind.

- *Building relationships.* Community is nurtured through the creation and sustaining of relationships of trust and support.

- *Leadership.* Committed and capable lay and ordained leaders need to articulate God's call and inspire a congregation to act.

- *Spiritual growth.* Members of the congregation continue to grow and mature in faith through spiritual practices.

- *Servanthood.* A spirit of serving and compassionate care must permeate the congregation.

- *Awareness of context.* A real knowledge of the environment and context is important, gained through both formal and informal means of conversation.

- *Hopeful proclamation.* Good preaching and other means of gospel proclamation offer an essential message of hope.

- *Stewardship.* Teaching and practicing sacrificial giving is a way of seeking God's kingdom first.

- *Hospitality and evangelism.* A climate of invitation and welcome is needed, with an intentional process of evangelism and recruitment.

♦ *Excellent programs.* Whether few or many, programs should be well planned and engage people's lives and hopes.

♦ *Dynamic worship.* Worship must engage the worshiper with hope, transformation, and spirit.

♦ *Streamlined structure.* There should be enough organization to get the work done but not so much as to stifle the spirit.

♦ *Vision for the future.* A congregation needs dreams for the future and plans to implement those dreams.

These characteristics illustrate the dimensions of congregational life that embody the theology and practice of mission. Baptismal practice, identity, and awareness transform the teaching, worship, and service experience of the congregation. The local community of faith itself realizes that it is a community of transformation for people who are a part of it and others who can be invited. It is a congregation that seeks to be an instrument of transformation in the world, a community of faith assisting people who experience great change and transition in their own lives. In these communities there is a clear awareness that the Holy Spirit is at work leading, guiding, directing, and strengthening it for mission, as people are being transformed in their own experiences of God and life. Scriptural stories of and witnesses to transformation are the focus and foundation of church life.

The mission of the Church is to restore all people to unity with God and each other in Christ. *(BCP 855)*

We simply cannot pursue our mission with the assumptions of previous generations. Rather, we must engage congregational life and work in new ways. The church is called to transformation and to being an agent of transformation in the world. To do this it must change. It must be transformed through its encounter with scripture and theology, and through its encounter with the Holy Spirit. This transformation is happening in many communities of faith in the Episcopal Church, but it needs to happen with even greater frequency. It is an urgent and hopeful moment.

"Shall we gather at the river?" That is the question asked of every community of faith. It is a question about Holy Baptism, about coming to the waters of grace and love. It is also a question about being a church that is willing to navigate the waters of change and transition that are all around us in our culture today. It is a question about change, about whether we are willing to be transformed by the power of God. And so it is to the dynamics of change and transformation that we turn next.

chapter two

Whitewater
Conditions

I will never forget the impact Michael Ramsey made on
all of us when he arrived at the seminary where I was a
student. What a remarkable man! By then he had retired
as the Archbishop of Canterbury, but he brought with
him all of the things that had made him such an extraor-
dinary leader in his former role: humility, prayer, theological depth, reverence for scripture, and a keen sense of the
Christian community and its mission.

My first real encounter with Ramsey's theological writ-
ings did not take place then, however, but on the other
side of the Atlantic during my theological study there. *The
Glory of God and the Transfiguration of Christ* was for me
life-changing because it was so clearly a book about transformation. Michael Ramsey turned to the scriptural tradition, and particularly the account of Christ's
transfiguration, to present a theology of transformation
and glory. Human beings *can* be transfigured, he insisted;
we can experience the very glory of God. The transfiguration was not an isolated historical event occurring on a

mountaintop in the Holy Land two thousand years ago, but an ongoing dynamic of Christian faith and life.

Archbishop Ramsey described the direct effects of Christ's transfiguration on human beings in this way:

- Our suffering is transfigured.

- Our knowledge is transfigured.

- Our world is transfigured.

Life is not static nor is God remote, disconnected from our daily life. Rather, our relationship with God changes us, transforms and transfigures us. In similar fashion, the world is transformed and transfigured through God's presence and action. Archbishop Ramsey perceived that human suffering, while very real and challenging, is changed through the love of a God who willingly suffered on the cross. He also saw that the human mind was changed and transformed by God's action, and that even the world is changed through the transforming power of God. Archbishop Ramsey invited his readers to recognize this transformation and to live within its dynamics in individual lives and the mission of the church. "Since we are faced with a universe that seems both hostile and unrelenting in its destructiveness," he wrote, "Christian faith is not a panacea but a gospel of transfiguration." The one who is transfigured is "the Son of Man; and, as he disclosed on Mount Hermon another world, he reveals that no part of created things and no moment of created time lie outside the power of the Spirit, who is Lord, to change from glory to glory."[7]

Michael Ramsey's ministry stood at the beginning of the postmodern shift. He experienced the significant changes wrought by two destructive world wars and the social transitions following both of those conflicts. He served as Archbishop of Canterbury in the 1960s and 1970s when the traditional norms of religion and society were shifting all around him. He knew that Western progressive assumptions were being challenged every day. Ramsey also perceived in Holy Scripture that the power of change, transformation, and transfiguration was the work and purpose of God. Human beings were not simply victims of the change occurring around them. As scripture told the story, they were being changed by the power and love of God. Archbishop Ramsey's observations about transfiguration and transformation apply both to individual believers and to the church and its mission.

The core event of the Hebrew scriptures, the saga of God's people being freed from captivity and slavery in Egypt for freedom and new hope in their journey to the promised land, is a story of transformation. It is God's power, purpose, and mission that transform the Hebrew people from hopelessness to hope, from oppression to new beginnings, from slavery to freedom.

God's people experience transformation throughout their experience of their Creator and Redeemer. When they fall into sin and far away from God, God transforms them through forgiveness and restoration. When they find themselves in captivity after the destruction of their city, temple, and way of life, God ultimately changes their circumstances into restoration and return. They go home to Jerusalem to rebuild their lives, their tradition, and their place of worship. The Hebrew prophets call for transformation over and over again: "Change your hearts." "Return to the Lord." "Give up your oppression of the poor and the helpless." Thus God's people are consistently and continually called to be transformed. Sometimes they respond to that call with faith and responsible action; sometimes they feel too young (Samuel) or unworthy (Isaiah). At other times, they resist the transformation which God offers and fall into alienation and irresponsibility. God, however, transforms them so that they can live out God's mission and their own mission and call as well. Transformation itself is the nature of God's interaction with them and the call to mission which God enunciates to them. In every age men and women are invited to be transformed by God's action and will in their own lives, transformation that comes through prayer, worship, and following the covenant God made with our ancestors.

Jesus of Nazareth appears on the scene with the message of power and transformation. The people whom he invites and embraces are changed and transformed. It really is quite remarkable. Fishermen, tax collectors, warriors, harlots, poor and rich, women and men, children and young people are transformed by the message and action of Jesus' mission. The mission itself is one of transformation. He is out to bring in the radical change wrought by the sovereignty of God. Human transformation is effected through his mission of healing, preaching, hospitality, and life-giving grace.

Do not be conformed to this world, but be transformed by the renewing of your minds, so that you may discern what is the will of God—what is good and acceptable and perfect. (Romans 12:2)

Jesus' own transfiguration is a paradigm of transformation. He goes up to the mountain top and is radically transfigured and transformed there. The disciples, even through their confusion and sleepiness, witness a magnificent change in Jesus. They see him for who he truly is: God's Son, the Beloved. It is a wonderful story, but its import extends far beyond the mountaintop experience. It is a paradigm of the transformation that is part of the Christian faith and life. He is changed, and *we* are changed. He is transformed, and *we* are transformed. He is transfigured, and *we* are transfigured.

St. Paul was changed from an enemy and persecutor of the early Christian community to one of its leaders and champions. Two stories that narrate this change are close together in the Acts of the Apostles. In one, Saul (as he was previously called) stands by and even encourages the rabble as Stephen the first deacon is murdered right before his very eyes. In the second story, which occurs shortly thereafter, Saul is knocked down from his horse, blinded, and completely changed through an encounter with the Risen Christ. For that reason Paul calls for transformation to be an integral part of the Christian experience in his letters. Paul perceives that Christian faith and life are transformation. He sees it as a call to change and to be changed. Certainly Paul experienced this in his own journey of faith. It would be hard to portray a more serious and radical change of soul and heart than that experienced by this early apostle and leader.

Just as Paul discovered that transformation is at the heart of Christian faith, the early church as a whole witnessed great change and transformation. The very nature of that community changed as it became an entity with its own identity, separate from temple and syna-gogue. Change was the daily fare for that early community of believers. From the day of Pentecost to the ongoing experience of the early apostolic community, change was continuous.

Peter said, "If then God gave them the same gift that he gave us when we believed in the Lord Jesus Christ, who was I that I could hinder God?" When they heard this, they were silenced. And they praised God, saying, "Then God has given even to the Gentiles the repen-tance that leads to life." (Acts 11:17–18)

One particularly remarkable change was reflected in the experience of the apostle Peter. In a great and terri-fying dream, in which a tablecloth came down from heaven full of clean and unclean animals, his mind and heart were changed. God told him to eat foods that he had previously regarded as utterly and completely impure. The message was clear. Many of the things that had been considered impure and out of bounds in the previous structure of his religion were now acceptable through the love of God and the event of Christ's resurrection. What a change! All were invited to God's community, table, and love: Gentile, Jew, slave, free, women, and men.

Clearly, a theology of transformation, in which alienation and separation are transformed by the grace and power of God so that unity and restoration may be effected, is rooted in Holy Scripture. The mission, purpose, and work of God in the world as told in the scriptural witness is to transform the cosmos, the church, and individual human beings. Congregations are communities of transformation. Their work and mission is inextricably connected to transformation, to change. People are transformed through practices of faith they encounter in congregations, as Christians seek to transform and change the world into a fuller reflection of the love and sovereignty of God.

a theology of hope

A theology of transformation is a theology of hope. The human life and soul are transformed so that they may be joined to God and enjoy new life and hope. It recognizes the power of God at work in the world, in the church, in the local congregation, and in the human heart and soul. But transformation inevitably means change, and change is a complex experience of transition and loss as well as hope and renewal.

Educator and author Parker Palmer offers a useful perspective on change for all believers, leaders, and congregations. In his incisive essay "Leading from Within,"[8] he contrasts five "lights" and the brilliance of belief with the five "shadows" that keep us separated from God's grace and love. He identifies the shadows as:

1. Insecurity about identity and worth.

Transformation can elude us, because we do not believe that we are worthy of love from God and other human beings. We are insecure about the goodness that is at the very foundation of our identity by virtue of being God's children, and this insecurity contributes to conflict in congregations, inhibiting their capacity to be communities of transformation.

2. Believing that the universe is a battleground, hostile to human interests.

This shadow also inhibits human transformation. Its challenge is the sense that life is hostile, that there "isn't enough to go around," and that we cannot really trust much of anything or anyone. These dynamics keep the human soul paralyzed, prohibiting the transforming grace of trust, reconciliation, and peacemaking. This too has a negative effect on local communities of faith and larger expressions of the church. Much of the anger and conflict that we witness in the church today reflects this shadow. In the place of transforming community, we find pitched battles over ideas, practices, and tradition. Instead of living into the mission of restoration and reconciliation, we settle for hostility and distrust.

3. "Functional atheism," which believes that ultimate responsibility for life and its results rests with us.

I have always believed that this is the most serious of the shadows that Parker describes and is a particular challenge to the souls and churches of North American mainline Christians. It is the resistance to recognize the efficacy, presence, and action of God in our lives and the life of the church and the world. Somehow we do not believe that

God can really do what God promises. This has serious and deleterious results for believers and the church itself. We overwork and over-program to achieve the results we want, becoming fatigued and dispirited in the process. Barriers to the spirit replace openness to transformation and inner change in individuals and congregations.

4. Fearing the natural chaos of life.

This pervasive shadow is particularly prevalent in our time of massive transition. There is free-floating anxiety and fright as things change quickly and consistently in our present moment. Chaos often seems to reign. Individuals fear this chaos instead of being open to the transforming presence of God. Similarly, congregations become more rigid and inflexible out of fear of change rather than developing the flexibility and openness that allow them to move into the future without knowing all of the answers. Such inflexibility rooted in fear is one of the characteristics of congregations that are declining or not living into their potential.

5. Denial of death

In our society, we go to great lengths to avoid and deny death. We "cosmetize" and mask it. This is the very antithesis of the basic tenet of the Christian faith which holds that life and resurrection come from death. Death is not to be avoided (nor can it be avoided). Rather, death is transformed by God's power and love to become life. Individuals cannot come to the fullness of the gift of life by refusing to grapple with human mortality and finality. Congregations cannot come to the realities of vitality and new life without engaging the shadows of loss, death, and grief.

These five shadows can inhibit our transformation and paralyze our souls. However, Palmer believes that the light is stronger, and that we can access that transforming light in our own inner beings, calling upon the transformation that God is creating within us.

> If we are to cast less shadow and more light, we need to ride certain monsters all the way down, explore the shadows they create, and experience the transformation that can come as we "get into" our own spiritual lives. —Parker Palmer

In Parker Palmer's view, each of the shadows is met by light, light that transforms the human soul and communities of faith. These are the transforming gifts of:

1. Security in our identity as beloved children of God.

We know our identity and are secure in it. The foundation of that identity is the love that God has for us and the infinite worth which is ours by virtue of creation by a loving God. Every congregation is a community centered around this basic identity, nurturing and transforming people in the awareness of our own identity as beloved daughters and sons of their Creator.

2. Participation in the empowering Shalom of God.

We recognize that God is the God of Shalom, of powerful and encompassing peace. We are invited to enter and dwell in that Shalom, to be transformed and strengthened by it. We can participate as individuals and as communities of faith. This is a theological reality that finds expression in practices of peacemaking, reconciliation and generosity.

3. Faith and trust in the efficacy and action of God.

We recognize the power of God in the world and in our own lives. We do not have to make everything happen or pretend that we are in charge of our own destinies. God has the potency to do what God promises to do. For individuals this means the discovery of the capacity for personal mission and ministry which resides in our souls. For a congregation this means that there needs to be an awareness of God's activity and direction in congregational life and mission. Congregations are called to envision new possibilities and take new risks for the gospel.

4. Love that transforms and replaces fear.

When we perceive that we are loved by our Creator, Redeemer, Sustainer God, then hope replaces fear. Possibility replaces anxiety. This is a theology of transformation rooted in love. We know that God's basic characteristic is creative, redemptive, and restoring love, and that knowledge allows us to overcome our fear with freedom and hope. This is a particularly important theological and spiritual reality for congregations. Survival, fear of context, suspicion of change can be transformed into love that exhibits itself in vital community life and service.

5. Resurrection hope and vitality.

We know that God is the God of life. Death is real, and cannot be avoided. However, the life of God is even stronger. The promise of resurrection and life gives us strength in the present and transforms our lives into greater vitality. A primary tenet of the Christian faith is the resurrection itself, and a primary experience of congregational life can be resurrection where people encounter life and vitality.

◆　◆　◆　◆　◆

Palmer's ten points capture foundational beliefs about God, humanity, and the community of faith. His is a profoundly practical theology in which people and communities can be moved away from the shadows that paralyze them to new light, new trust, and new love. His theology of transformation provides a realistic approach to the world and human nature. There is sadness, human sinfulness, violence, and war in this world and in ourselves. We do live in the shadows in our own existence, but the gift of transformation is at work here as well. The cross of Jesus Christ stands in the midst of the challenging realities of human existence. The cross itself is a sign of the solidarity of God with us in all of our frailties, vulnerabilities, and sorrows. The cross is a sign of the transforming power God in the face of the shadows which we face.

whitewater conditions

Congregations likewise experience transformation and change as both light and shadow, renewal and loss. Local communities of faith are like other institutions and organizations in our society. They experience rapid, unrelenting change, change which—to return to our image of the baptismal waters of transformation—is fast flowing and churning. Leadership educator and writer Peter Vaill uses the expression "permanent whitewater" to describe the "complex, turbulent, changing environment in which we are all trying to operate." These are the intertwining characteristics of this continuous, indeed "permanent" whitewater change:

1. Permanent whitewater conditions are full of surprises.

We know that from our experience in mission and congregational life. Something that we did not expect will suddenly present itself as a challenge. It may be an opportunity for mission that we could not anticipate such as a new demographic in our community, or it may be a problem that had not occurred in the past but reflects new patterns of life in American culture and society.

2. Complex systems tend to provide novel problems.

Everything just seems more complicated than it used to. One congregation recently sought to invite new neighbors to its parish life, only to discover that communication was very complex in an area where a "gated" entrance was the norm for housing. Another calls a new priest only to discover that the spouse was not at all willing to make the move.

3. Whitewater events are often extremely costly.

How much does it take to provide yearly financial support for a local congregation? Churches must be kept up to building codes; as church buildings age, deferred maintenance becomes a burning question. There are massive adjustments in congregational finances as patterns of giving change for all Americans. The costs of health and property insurance have skyrocketed. To provide a just and suitable compensation for clergy is much more expensive in the present environment.

4. Permanent whitewater conditions raise the problem of recurrence.

If it's not one thing, then it's another. Many boards or vestries of congregations are suffering real fatigue at this point. The effects of change are recurrent and cumulative. There are personnel, program, and financial decisions that continually present themselves and congregations and conditions change.[9]

All of us have been on this particular river. We experience the surprises and "messiness" described by Peter Vaill in institutions and organizations of all sorts, large and small, sacred and secular. An illusion found in many congregations, their members, and their leaders is that congregational life and experience will be stable, consistent, and "clean." Sometimes nostalgia presents itself, longing for a time in the past when the dynamics of calm were normative. Probably they never were.

Be that as it may, calm, cool, and collected congregational life is not the norm today. Vaill's analysis of institutions holds true for congregations. There are surprises and novel problems. Things simply are not like they used to be. You cannot count on the same stream of financial support. New people show up and expect new things: more adult programs, more youth work, more spirituality, a different preaching style, a better physical plant. There are novel problems in leadership, planning, and even relationship to communities and context. Often it seems "messy," and congregational leaders sometimes wish for more structure and stability. Everything costs more, and many congregations feel that they are ready to sink in the seas of financial insolvency. Yes, church communities today, like the legal, business, and medical communities, are surging down the whitewater.

We experience whitewater change in our personal lives as well. We live in a fast moving, constantly changing world and life. Things on which we used to count for stability—our families, institutions, workplaces, associations, towns, schools, churches—are not as stable and secure today. Part of this huge shift (commonly called the postmodern shift) around us is lack of certainty about traditions, ethics, and meaning. Today we find ourselves in a great quest for meaning and for narratives that can give us a solid and stable foundation in our lives.

William Bridges, one of the best analysts in the areas of transition and change, has described change and its psychological effects in his writing during the past several years. Although we are living through a vast volume of transition in our own lives and in institutions and organizations, he observes, such transitions have benefits. They move us from one place to another, through the ending of something to the beginning of something new. Bridges defines transition as "the process of letting go of the way things used to be and then taking hold of the way they subsequently become." He goes on to note: "It is a paradox: to achieve continuity we have to be willing to change. Change is in fact the only way to protect whatever exists, for without continuous readjustment, the present cannot continue."[10]

So these are the lives and the experiences that we bring to church. As a pastor, I have been with people in the midst of their changes and transitions. Some of them are happy and mark new beginnings in life: marriages and other significant lifelong relationships, welcoming people to new communities, the birth or adoption of children, going to school, joining new groups, entering new professions and phases of profession. Some changes are challenging and mark difficult transitions: the loss of a job, moving away from a much loved community, a divorce, the death of someone who is dear, going to war. People bring all of these transitions to church with them. As the following aspects of change in twenty-first century churches show, the congregation is a community of faith and a community of multiple transitions.

CULTURE

The church is in a different cultural position than was previously the case. In American life today we find ourselves on the margins of culture and society in a variety of ways. We compete with many other things that claim attention and participation in our culture.

> *Example:* While interviewing a group of new church planters in a southern state and diocese, we heard stories of success and vital new communities of faith. I asked the question: "What has been your greatest challenge?" To which they replied in unison one word, "SOCCER!" I was amazed. I had expected responses naming financial constraints, diocesan poli-

tics, leadership fatigue and the like. What I got was a surprise. Here were congregations that had to compete for attention and participation in a cultural context known as the "Bible Belt," a context where just a couple of generations ago people could not even go to a store or mow their lawns or play baseball on a Sunday.

MEMBERSHIP
Ideas and styles of membership have changed in American society. Membership is down in many organizations, and it is down in the church as well. People participate in a variety of ways, but they are reluctant to "join."

> *Example:* One congregation in the Episcopal Church surprised its local bishop when he visited. He confirmed a good number of people in this vital and growing congregation and welcomed them as members of the congregation and wider church. He was then ready to go on with the service, but the rector stopped him and said, "Wait, bishop. There are others for you to bless, those who are not ready to join this congregation and be confirmed but who want your blessing because they find meaning and community here." Three times the number of those being confirmed stood up and received this blessing of relationship rather than joining.

SPIRITUALITY
People are interested in spirituality and spiritual experience, but this interest does not automatically translate into participation or desire for involvement in religious organizations.

> *Example:* It happened again on an airplane not too long ago. A young man asked me what I did for a living, to be going overseas at that particular time. "I

am an Episcopal Church priest," I answered. He then described his life and faith: "Well, I am spiritual and pray every day, and I have a number of friends that do that too. But none of us go to church. We just don't know what it's about, and we've never really been invited...."

EVANGELISM

Evangelism and recruitment are of the essence for congregations today. People simply will not "show up" formed in other Christian traditions so that they might be "Episcopalian-ized."

> *Example:* During a recent vestry meeting at Our Savior Episcopal Church, some members of the vestry challenged the rector regarding his interest in evangelism. "Don't you care about us anymore?" they asked. "Why are you spending all this time with new people? What about the oldsters?" These and other questions were articulated by long-time church members. Underneath them all were two major concerns. First, these parish leaders were unhappy that there needed to be intentional evangelism and recruitment. In the "old days" the right kind of people simply showed up. Second, those who *did* find the parish at present were not people with whom the veteran leaders felt comfortable. The newcomers seemed to know little about the church and its heritage.

CHRISTIAN TRADITION

Since people have not grown up in a Christian culture, they do not know the stories and narratives of the Christian tradition.

> *Example:* "Who came first, Moses or Jesus?" "I hate to admit it, but I have never owned a Bible." "I have

never been in a church before, even for a wedding or a funeral." "My high school used to have a baccalaureate service but the courts stopped that several years ago." These are actual statements I have heard reflecting the present context and culture where people no longer have a foundation in Christian culture and story. It is not a part of our cultural narrative or milieu any longer.

STEWARDSHIP

The giving patterns of American people have changed. We are less likely to give in an ongoing "pledging" pattern and more likely to give to special projects and areas of focus. This is especially the case with younger generations of Americans.

> *Example:* At a meeting of Episcopal congregations with the responsibility and blessing of endowment resources, the churches' stewardship directors were lamenting the fact that it is harder and harder to make budget income goals through annual giving campaigns and canvasses. One of their number agreed and described the story of a younger couple who gave a modest annual gift but responded affirmatively to the request for a special project to enhance the youth ministry... to the tune of $250,000.

EXPECTATIONS

It is harder for small congregations to do their work now in the same way they have done it in the past. American people expect a wide range of choices in church programs and will "shop" for the congregation that will meet their desire to learn and their personal spiritual needs.

> *Example:* The vestry of St. John's Church has been struggling for two years. They just can't make the

budget balance anymore. They used to be able to afford a full-time priest, care for the building, and operate a couple of good programs, but not now. This congregation is not in a small community, and there are other churches in the area. Members of the vestry have watched three families come and go in the last year: these people came to their congregation for a while, enjoyed the congregational life, but then "moved on" to a congregation that could offer more in terms of music, education, or outreach.

DENOMINATIONAL LOYALTY
Denominational loyalty cannot be taken for granted. There is an interest in tradition and identity coming from a particular denominational heritage and experience, but there is also general suspicion of denominational structures.

Example: John and Suzi were not active in a local congregation in their single years in college and post-college. Now they are married, have a child, and want to attend a church. Believe it or not, they were both brought up as Episcopalians so when they decided it was time to attend a church, they visited an Episcopal Church first. But they kept on shopping until they found what they were looking for, because program was more important to them than denominational affiliation.

POPULATION LOSS
Rural areas and small towns continue to lose population, particularly younger generations.

Example: St. Paul's Church is in a beautiful rural community where there used to be seventy-five hundred people. Now there are barely three thousand. The state government has just begun an initiative to try to hold on to young college graduates, since the state's present retention rate is the second lowest for any state in the Union. The congregation continues to decline in membership and to "gray" in the age of its members.

MORALITY

There is greater diversity in perspectives on moral and ethical issues and on biblical use and interpretation.

Example: St. Paul's Church is a larger congregation in a midwestern city. It is declining in membership after several years of growth for a number of reasons, not the least of which is a series of conflicts over contemporary ethical issues and the Bible's teaching. Where there used to be "agreement to disagree," today there is greater polarization and some loss of spirit and affection within the congregation.

LEADERSHIP

Expectations of lay and ordained leadership have changed, with greater possibilities for and demands on both groups. Clergy roles are less clearly defined and understood than in the past.

Example: St. Mary's Church has had a protracted controversy between its vestry and priest. They just don't understand each other. The vestry accused the priest of being distant and authoritarian, while he feels he is misunderstood and unfairly scrutinized. St. Mary's used to have a tradition of fairly long-term ordained leaders, but not anymore. It looks like the present priest might well leave after a little less than three years, just like his two predecessors.

AUTHORITY
Hierarchical authority has yielded to invitation and mutuality in church leadership.

Example: People were not too sure about it at first, but they love it now. The parish priest at Advent Church has invited people to join in several processes of leadership education, discernment, and empowerment. She had the vestry go on a retreat for the first time in years and has launched a process of vestry learning and education. Her leadership style has been described as "invitational" and "consensus building," a style different from the more hierarchical approach in the past.

WORSHIP
New forms of worship are emerging, and new forms of music necessitate change in the Sunday morning experience.

Example: It's not just the Prayer Book and *Hymnal 1982* at Trinity Church anymore. This congregation has recently introduced multimedia worship that includes prayers from the *New Zealand Prayer Book* and the *Enriching Our Worship* resources, as well as music from a variety of sources in America and beyond. The result has been a growth in attendance and the presence of younger people.

BAPTISMAL MINISTRY
New modes of training for lay and ordained leadership are found widely in the church, reflecting the new vision of baptismal ministry and necessitated by the rising costs of traditional ordination training.

Example: Christ Church, a rural congregation, has gone for several years without a full-time priest. At first there was embarrassment about it and a lot of wishing for the "good old days." The congregation also continued a slow but unyielding decline in its membership. Then the congregation got a new vision. It envisioned ministry and leadership that would be done by a team specially prepared for this work. There was a growing sense of hope, not loss, and a realization that this was a form of ministry rooted in baptismal covenant and identity. This congregation is experiencing much hope and has introduced a major new ministry of compassion within its small community.

DIVERSITY
Our society is increasingly diverse in all sorts of ways, including multicultural and multiracial.

Example: Holy Spirit Church had long been a small Anglo congregation in a major city. The members of the congregation had long been aware that there were few people like themselves in the neighborhood anymore. But then they noticed something else: hundreds of the new people in the neighborhood were Hispanic. So they began a parallel service in Spanish. It grew rapidly. Now the neighborhood has changed again, as more middle and higher income people (both Hispanic and Anglo) are moving in. The congregation continues its learning about welcoming new people who are "different."

enhancing congregational strength

In the midst of these whitewater shifts and changes in church and culture, how do congregations become communities of transformation? What do we know about the concrete practices and attitudes that enhance congregational mission? What are the qualities and characteristics of effective congregations?

Studies of congregations and congregational development have been full and promising during the past several years, providing useful and helpful information for local congregations and their leaders about ways to enhance congregational life and mission. Two of these lenses for congregational assessment are the Faith Communities Today (FACT) survey and the U.S. Congregational Life Survey.

THE FAITH COMMUNITIES TODAY SURVEY

The Faith Communities Today survey, studying many denominations and thousands of congregations in the United States, has been done twice in the last few years, first in 2001 and more recently in 2005. A congregational survey sent to leaders of local communities of faith in several major denominations, it gathered information about trends in congregations and their ministry and mission. Dr. Kirk Hadaway, the Episcopal Church's Director of Research, worked with other denominational researchers to frame and analyze the survey's results, particularly focusing on the Episcopal Church and its congregations. Through the survey's questions about mission, demographics, practices, and theology we have learned a great deal about our congregations both in terms of their basic identity and of how they function in the midst of the changes described above. This picture of Episcopal congregations offers important perspectives on congregational life, mission, and change.

Three statements in the FACT survey were particularly revealing and correlated with congregational strength when respondents indicated a high level of agreement with these statements as they examined the life of their own congregation:

   ♦ "Our congregation is spiritually vital and alive."

♦ "Our congregation helps members deepen their relationship with God."

♦ "We have a clear sense of mission and purpose."

So even in our present confusion, we can see that strong congregations are focused on mission and purpose. They know what they are about and have done the work of examining and articulating their mission. Strong congregations also are communities of change and renewal where people experience spiritual transformation as deep relationship with God and spiritual vitality. Diana Butler Bass has noted in her recent book *The Practicing Congregation* that strong congregations are intentional: they use practices and disciplines reflecting the core identity of the congregation's mission and transforming human beings in faith. Butler Bass provides an extensive description of such "practicing congregations" as "communities that choose to rework denominational tradition in light of local experience to create a web of practices that transmit identity, nurture community, cultivate mature spirituality, and advance mission."[11]

The FACT survey offers other descriptions of Episcopal congregations today as well. The largest percentage of Episcopal congregations is small churches, but very few congregations are to be found in rural and open country areas. The majority of Episcopal congregations are found in metropolitan areas and towns, but we have lagged in founding congregations in new suburbs. The FACT survey reports that Episcopalians value worship and Episcopal identity highly. Eucharistic worship is an essential ingredient of Episcopal identity and experience, "filled with God's presence, participatory, and welcoming to newcomers."

The parochial report summary, reported with the FACT survey, also shows that half of Episcopal congregations have been declining in average Sunday attendance and membership during the past three years (as have 89 percent of dioceses). This contrasts with the Episcopal Church's state in the 1990s, when we were stable or even slightly growing as a denomination. Younger generations are seriously underrepresented in the Episcopal Church when compared to their percentage in the general population, while the percentage of Episcopalians sixty-five years of age and older is over twice the percentage of the American population as a whole. Minority populations are also underrepresented in the Episcopal Church.

Essentially the Episcopal Church is facing the same challenges of membership, attendance, and decline as other denominations. So this trend is not about theology, or about liberal versus conservative attitudes per se. Rather it is the result of the forces of change I have outlined earlier, changes that are sweeping through our culture and through American religion itself. Our present decline is the result of changing patterns of religious affiliation and demographics. It is "systemic decline" and calls for the intentional response of evangelism.[12]

Responses for the FACT survey indicated that congregations express a clear desire to grow in membership, but a distinct minority of Episcopal churches have intentional recruitment programs and evangelism strategies. Various factors correlate with the vitality and strength of congregations, and they will be described in greater detail in a future chapter. At this point, it is sufficient to highlight the FACT survey's basic learning that vital worship, intentional evangelism, spiritual transformation, caring community, and a learning emphasis correlate with congregational strength. Leadership is also important. The FACT survey portrays Episcopal clergy who are good pastors and liturgists but who do not rate as highly in strategy, evangelism, and leadership. Obviously this presents huge challenges to our future. Our congregations need to be focused on mission, invitation, and spiritual transformation.

The results of the FACT survey identify several things that contribute to congregational growth and vitality. They include:

> ◆ *Spiritual transformation:* the ongoing experience of spiritual transformation that joins people closer to God in their faith and living.

People go to church and become part of a local congregation because of their desire encounter God and spiritual experience. The congregations that offer structures, opportunities, and practices for spiritual transformation reflect other dynamics of vitality and growth.

> ◆ *Clarity of mission and purpose:* clear understanding of the basic values, actions and purpose of a congregation with particular focus on mission.

A congregation which knows what it is about and is able to communicate that reality in inviting and compelling ways also reflects dynamics of vitality and growth. Congregations that do not know their basic call and mission or who mask this reality with a proliferation of programs are not as inviting.

> ◆ *New housing:* the presence of new units of housing in both urban and suburban settings.

This might be new single family housing in suburbs or newly built or renovated multiple family housing in cities. It is particularly important for local congregations to know what is happening in their community at this moment. Oftentimes assumptions are made based on outdated information, and a congregation can actually miss the growth and new community life around it.

◆ *New people:* new populations that have moved into a suburban or urban area and the presence of new people in a local congregation itself.

As with new housing, it is possible for a congregation to miss new people, because existing members are looking for people who look like themselves, even though the local community is no longer populated by that demographic. Dynamic congregations enter their local communities and do the research to see just who is moving in and has settled into a community. New people are often in the midst of multiple transitions in their own lives, when they are open to or looking for invitations to a community of faith.

◆ *Younger families:* congregations that include younger families and that are located in communities where young families live reflect a readiness for invitation and potential growth for congregations.

Young families are a perfect example of people who are in transition and a particular time of searching and seeking. Congregations that invite and respond to the needs of younger families grow in a variety of ways. The efforts spent in community nursery programs, preschools, excellent Christian formation programming, and family life education bear good results for the young families and for the growth of congregations. The percentage of younger people in a congregation actually correlates with the growth of the congregation itself.

◆ *Marriage, parenting, and family programs:* learning that connects to the real and daily living of people, particular those with children.

More will be said about the learning environment of the local congregation, but this discovery in the Faith Communities Today survey gives more specificity to the type of Christian education that directly connects to people (especially younger families) and the important issues and experiences of their daily living.

⬧ *A learning environment:* congregational life in which learning is taken seriously, joyfully, and regularly.

Learning for people of all ages is at the heart of congregational vitality. It indicates openness and a hopeful spirit of inquiry in a local congregation. Most importantly it roots people in formation around their own identity and spiritual experiences.

⬧ *Intentional recruitment:* a stated vision and action plan to invite, welcome, and incorporate new people into congregational life.

Almost every congregation expresses a desire to grow, but a far smaller percentage organize themselves to do it. Growing and vital congregations develop intentional plans of evangelism and recruitment.

⬧ *Joyful worship:* spirit and joy in corporate worship and in preaching.

You can discern the spiritual climate of most congregations within the first twenty minutes of public worship and preaching. Dynamic congregations have dynamic worship and preaching that portray the joy of the gospel and suggest that something life-changing is happening here.

⬧ *Fuller churches and more services:* Sunday morning worship that does not look empty, and the offering of more and different styles of worship.

Change the seating, utilize a different room, do whatever is necessary so that your Sunday morning worship does not look empty. Growing congregations have refined the ability to have their worship space full enough and not too full. They also use multiple services and different styles of services to invite new people.

♦ *Clergy stability and tenure:* longer term service by clergy where trust and vision are built together.

Leadership is of the essence for strong congregations. (Both clergy and lay leadership.) Optimal clergy leadership is the leadership that has served for a few years in a local congregation while still remaining fresh to new ideas and opportunities.

♦ *Resolution of conflict:* the intentional negotiation and resolution of conflict whenever it emerges in congregational life.

It is not the absence of conflict that marks healthy and strong congregational life. It is the management of the conflict. Vital congregations acknowledge disagreement and use appropriate means for negotiation and resolution.

♦ *Flexibility:* the willingness to try new things and flexibly meet new challenges.

Congregations that reflect hope and openness to new ideas, strategies, people, and opportunities are strong and growing. Rigidity impairs a congregation and, in some instances, paralyzes it.

♦ *"A fun place to be":* a climate of hope and celebration.

This relates to joyful worship and preaching, but is even broader than that. Congregations which were identified as fun places to be in the FACT survey showed other indicators of strength. Who wants to go to church where it is dreary and "no fun"?

♦   ♦   ♦   ♦   ♦

No congregation does all of these things or does them equally well. This learning shows that there are certain characteristics and marks of congregational life that make a difference in terms of vitality and growth. They also contribute to the potential for growth.

THE U.S. CONGREGATIONAL LIFE SURVEY

Like the Faith Communities Today survey, the U.S. Congregational Life Survey, funded by the Lilly Endowment, provides an important perspective on the life of congregations in the United States. It was completed by fewer Episcopal congregations than the FACT survey but by many more individuals. Rather than surveying congregational leaders only, the U.S. Congregational Life Survey employed a method of seeking responses from numerous congregational participants. Some 41,000 Episcopalians completed the survey in Sunday morning congregational settings.

The U.S. Congregational Life Survey describes a great deal about American congregational life. Dr. Cynthia Woolever of Hartford Seminary has been the overall director of the survey. Dr. Kirk Hadaway, Director of Research in the Episcopal Church, and Dr. Matthew Price, Director of Research for the Church Pension Fund, have been the two responsible parties for research within the Episcopal Church and its congregations. They will eventually publish a full analysis of the research and its description of Episcopal congregational life.

Learning about congregational transformation and vitality abounds in the U.S. Congregational Life Survey results. Some of the qualities of congregational transformation described in the survey include:

> • *Providing a sense of community:* fellowship and mutuality experienced in the life of the congregation.

People have too few experiences of community in our fast-paced American style of life. In this survey, respondents described the importance of community experience as a foundation for their involvement in a congregation. Stronger congregations reflected vibrant community life.

♦ *Strong morale:* the recognition of congregational strengths and operating from those strengths.

There are plenty of challenges and issues for congregations today. However, the congregations which possessed strong and high morale are able to meet those challenges.

♦ *Excitement about the future:* a hopeful sense regarding the congregation's future and potential.

A congregation which communicates excitement about God's future and its own future is able to develop greater hope in individuals as well. It also recognizes the opportunities that are before it and bases its decisions on strengths rather than problems or weaknesses.

♦ *Seeks to educate worshipers about the faith:* a learning community for all ages.

Like the FACT survey, the U.S. Congregational Life Survey identified the importance of the learning climate and community.

♦ *Members share faith and invite others to attend:* a spirit of witness, invitation, and welcome.

This is about active recruitment on the part of a congregation and its individual members. People are able to tell their own faith stories and invite other people to attend their congregation's worship and/or special events.

♦ *Conveys the sense that life has meaning:* drawing a strong connection between gospel hope and personal life.

The great postmodern question is the question of meaning. Vital congregations offer a community for people to do reflection on the meaning of their lives in a fast-moving contemporary world, and they communicate a sense of meaning and hope for people's lives.

* *Willingness to try something new:* innovation, creativity, and new ventures.

This is the same dynamic as the flexibility described in the FACT survey. Vital congregations reflect an attitude of imagination and risk that leads them to attempt new ventures and create new vision.

* *Good match between members and ordained leader:* mutuality and good relationship between clergy and laity.

The higher the sense of match, the more satisfaction appears for clergy and lay members alike. Satisfaction leads to effective mission.

* *Serving others:* the congregation is not seen as an end in itself but as a servant community.

Vital congregations do tend to their own life and community to be sure, *and* they serve those in greatest need in the wider community.

* *Experience of "inspiration, mystery, and awe" in worship:* worship that is transcendent.

The FACT survey observes the importance of joyful transformation in worship. The U.S. Congregational Life Survey made a similar discovery about transcendent and transforming worship.

* *Population growth in zipcode area:* growing communities help to grow churches.

Growth of populations can happen in urban and suburban communities. Vital and growing congregations intentionally examine and connect with that growth.

* *Conflict resolution:* willingness to work through conflict and not let congregational life be dominated by it.

Festering conflict is one of the most destructive things to congregational life, mission, and evangelism. Resolution is the hard and rewarding work of intentionally addressing conflict.

* *Spiritual growth:* transformation and growth for members.

There are numerous opportunities for spiritual growth in vital congregations. It is not left to chance or to one particular style of worship.

The U.S. Congregational Life Survey gives a useful portrait of the life and characteristics related to congregational vitality and growth. Joined with the learning from the Faith Communities Today survey, they provide a picture of congregational strength.

◆　◆　◆　◆　◆

So . . . what do these findings mean for your congregation, as you seek to become a community of transformation? What should be the areas of focus for congregational strength, growth, and vitality? In the following chapters we will identify those areas and suggest modes of action that will allow your congregation to move forward in enhanced and strengthened mission.

The Vital Congregation

In chapters three and four we will look more closely at some of the characteristics of vital, healthy, and growing congregations described in chapter two. These marks of strong, effective congregations are supported by various learnings from research and practice. No congregation does all of them superbly, although many congregations excel in several of the areas. When a congregation decides it is time to assess its vitality and to make real changes in its life and mission, it is helpful for the leadership in the congregation to use these areas as a template for their reflection and conversation.

In this chapter we lay the foundations for becoming a vital and growing congregation: the essential work of clarifying mission; being a place of spiritual transformation; becoming aware of the surrounding context and congregational dynamics; the importance of learning and education; and focusing on evangelism and welcome.

clarifying mission

As we have seen, the twenty-first century is the "mission age" for congregational life and ministry, theologically and practically. One of the primary characteristics of vitality for congregations is the mission focus and clarity to be found within that congregation. Theology and practice must be joined together in strong congregations where the mission comes first.

This does not happen without intentional care and attention. Every congregation, and particularly its leadership, must pay attention to the understanding and articulation of its mission. Some of this is theological and biblical work, requiring the consideration of the themes of mission from Holy Scripture and doing theological reflection on the meaning of mission in the life and ministry of God's people. Some of this work roots the mission of the local congregation in wider understandings of mission, be it the Baptismal Covenant or the broad definition found in the Book of Common Prayer "to restore all people to unity with God and each other in Christ" (BCP 855).

Attention to mission also involves very specific and particular work emerging out of the experience of the local congregation. Good structures are available to help a congregation in doing this work. The framework of Appreciative Inquiry assists the congregation and its leaders to understand mission by identifying the strengths of the congregation and the patterns of strength that reflect the congregational mission. Other resources exist for mission definition and articulation for the congregation and its vestries.

Three dimensions of mission mirror God's presence and action over time: the past mission, the present mission, and the future mission. To understand the unique mission of a given congregation, it is essential for leaders to spend time considering all three.

THE PAST MISSION

A congregation needs to understand its past mission since the time of its founding. The identification of historically significant people and events allows present leaders to understand how mission has emerged and developed over time. This is essential to understanding and defining the present mission. History has power in the present, and every congregation is shaped by the decisions and vision of the congregation in its history. Whole congregations can reflect on their history through times of intentional learning and celebration.

THE PRESENT MISSION

The present mission of the congregation is the embodiment of its values and actions in the present moment. Different congregations have different identities and expressions of mission because of the unique realities of their own values and actions. Values are the enabling beliefs that inspire the congregation to service and actions. A cluster of these values are at work in every congregation. They may be values of learning or lively worship or compassionate outreach. They may be values of inclusion or vigorous invitation or close, nurturing community. Values are at the very foundation of congregational life, and, to understand mission, the congregation must connect with and understand these values, the things that are "precious" to them, as leadership scholar Ronald Heifetz puts it in his book *Leadership Without Easy Answers*.

The second part of the present mission work, then, is to connect a congregation's values to its actions. Is there alignment and resonance between the things that a congregation identifies as possessing great value and significance for them and the actions of the congregational life and program? Sometimes there is an unfortunate disconnect. At other times, there is a proliferation of congregational programs at the expense of effectiveness. Congregations try to do too much, doing programs that are not rooted in core values or doing such a great number of programs that the congregation's human and financial resources become exhausted. Conversely, when there is resonance and alignment between values and actions, powerful mission can occur within the congregation.

Leaders in the congregation have the special charge of reflection on present mission, its values, and its actions. They need to invite the wider congregation into that reflection, though. Some congregations opt to utilize learning presentations of the present mission so that the wider congregation can be aware and help to shape the mission.

THE FUTURE MISSION

The third dimension of mission lies in the future. A congregation's mission will proceed into the future, and the present mission lays a foundation for the future. Leaders in a congregation need to dream the dreams for the future and spend intentional time envisioning that future. Congregations can do this in different ways and using different processes. Good visioning resources exist and serve congregational leadership in envisioning a hopeful future and beginning the planning and strategy necessary to enter that future.

◆ ◆ ◆ ◆ ◆

Mission is composed of all three of these dimensions and directions. The essential thing for a congregation is to reflect, focus, and articulate mission rather than to be distracted by the numerous changes and issues that emerge in parish life. Yes, issues need to be addressed, but even more important is the mission work. Congregations that do this work and focus on their mission are stronger, more resilient, and more able to deal with the inevitable conflict that will occur from time to time.

1. How is your congregation doing this mission reflection, definition, and articulation?

2. In what ways are your congregational leaders spending intentional and consistent time working through all three dimensions of mission?

3. How well are your congregation's members able to describe the primary mission and identity of your congregation? (Mission is more than a "mission statement," but a clear articulation of mission that is understood and used by congregational members is helpful. The important thing is this. You understand the mission, remain focused on it, and use it as a compass for the progress of the congregation's life and ministry.)

4. Have you used appropriate external consultation to assist in this focus on mission clarity and purpose?

A CONGREGATION'S STORY

St. John's Church was basically a happy and whole community of faith. It had served its community for almost 150 years and had known many seasons of life and mission. Its town was not large, but it was the regional center of medical and other services for the area. Averaging around 180 worshipers each week, it enjoyed financial health and good community visibility. St. John's offered a number of programs, although many of them seemed to be "running out of steam."

There was something nagging at the clergy and lay leadership of the congregation. Yes, they had basically good worship and there were no serious conflicts, but there seemed to be no real focus to what they were about. Neither congregational members nor people in the larger community could identify the core sense of purpose and identity for St. John's.

The clergy and wardens went to the diocesan annual clergy and wardens conference and heard a presentation about congregational mission, inviting them to do a process as leaders that would give them clarity about mission, a vision for the future, and the beginning of a strategy. They decided to use the consultation offered for their own mission and vision work.

The congregation's leaders (clergy, vestry, and some other key lay leaders) invested the time to look at all three directions in mission. What they discovered was of great use to them. They had a rich history, and they learned that past leaders had made some significant decisions that changed the focus of the congregation. They also learned that there had been some very challenging times when leadership had stepped up to the plate to refine and strengthen the congregation's mission. In their consideration of St. John's present mission, they reflected on the values and actions that were at the heart of their ministry. They also examined their community's demographic data and opportunities for mission and created surveys for their own congregational and community constituents. Finally, they envisioned the future for their congregation and began work on strategies and goals to live into that vision.

The result of this work was greater clarity about purpose and mission than St. John's had previously known. The clarity of mission made it easier to attract new lay leaders and volunteers. The new short and pithy mission statement they created became a focused articulation known by leaders and parish members. They began new initiatives, especially in evangelism and stewardship, and "retired" some programs that no longer served their needs. These efforts required a lot of work, to be sure, but a sense of energy and purpose permeated the parish life and culture. They were being transformed and became a more effective congregation of transformation in their community.

experiences of spiritual transformation

Vital congregations are communities where people can experience spiritual transformation. This happens in several different ways and through a variety of practices. People are transformed through intentional spiritual practices, through worship and prayer, through learning, through Christian community, and through compassionate service (to name some of the major avenues for transformation). The point is this: people yearn to experience a closer connection to and relationship with God.

Spiritual transformation is one of the primary purposes of the Christian church. A local congregation is at its very heart a community and system of such transformation. People come into the gathered community from their daily life and work in the world. They hear God's word, offer praise and prayer, learn together, and have experiences of Christian community. This, in turn, strengthens them for return to daily life and work where they live their ministry in a concrete and continuing way. It is a system of transformation, of change.

Every congregation needs to do an assessment of its life and programs in terms of spiritual transformation. It is not enough to offer something simply because of ongoing custom. In this day and age, offerings must possess spiritual dynamism and have the power to effect change.

1. *Worship.* Does your congregation's worship allow for silence as well as sound? Is there a joyful spirit that engages the worshiper's mind and heart?

2. *Preaching.* Is the preaching evocative and inviting for worship participants? Does it lift up Holy Scripture and connect its proclamation to daily life?

3. *Learning.* Are there sufficient learning opportunities in your congregation? Are they more than an intellectual endeavor (as important as the expression of the mind is), offering spiritual practice and content?

4. *Service and reflection.* Are there opportunities for service followed by reflection on the meaning of that experience?

5. *Spiritual practices.* Are spiritual practices encountered, taught, and encouraged?

6. *Encouragement for all ages.* Does the congregation offer spiritual enrichment for children, young people, and adults?

A CONGREGATION'S STORY

St. Timothy's is a small and lively congregation in the heart of an American city. It has been a financially supported congregation for decades. The building, built for a large congregation in the late nineteenth century, is far too big for the present average Sunday attendance of fifty people. Over the years the congregation has maintained regular worship and done a few, significant ministries of community service.

A new vicar appeared at St. Tim's who had a passion around spiritual formation and worship. She worked with a group of parishioners who had similar interests and began to develop worship and program offerings to introduce spiritual practices. The worship space itself was changed to be a more intimate and altar-focused setting. New forms of worship and music from the Iona and Taizé communities were introduced, along with expanded use of the liturgies in the Book of Common Prayer, *A New Zealand Prayer Book,* and *Enriching Our Worship.* Silence was employed in worship in an intentional way, and sermons were focused on spiritual growth and renewal.

The congregation began to learn about spiritual practices through reading and experimentation. One person introduced a centering prayer group that also practiced *lectio divina.* A study group read *Practicing Our Faith: A Way of Life for a Searching People* by Dorothy C. Bass and looked to see how these practices were experienced in their own lives and in the common life of the community. Connections to spiritual retreats and resources were offered in person and online as the congregation's website took a new form.

Today St. Tim's is a vital congregation that is just beginning to grow. Its growth is interesting in and of itself. Adults (and a few with children, but not many) have continued to be a part of the St. Timothy's community. There is a steady stream of adult visitors, but there is also a new group that has begun to show up in the congregation. Young adults, college students, recent graduates, and graduate/professional school students have arrived on the scene. Their point of intersection is the sense of spiritual inquiry and transformation that marks the congregation. The congregation is being transformed, and those who participate indicate that spiritual transformation is their primary reason for being present.

No congregation lives its life in a vacuum. Vital congregations are aware of this fact and seek to learn about the context and environment in which ministry takes place. These congregations also examine their own mission and life in light of learning offered regarding congregational dynamics.

There are several ways of learning more about context and environment for congregations and their leaders. Some of the most effective involve intentional and direct communication with people in their external community. Here are some that congregations have found particularly effective.

1. *Inviting community leaders and neighbors in.* A congregation can use regular program times like adult education for learning conversations with neighbors. Community representatives and leaders are brought to these occasions for presentation and conversation. Congregations also benefit from presentations by community organizations in these learning settings.

2. *Formal community surveys.* Models exist for congregations to prepare formal surveys to learn from neighbors, businesses, and community organizations. Less formal modes of community interaction and survey occur as congregational members are trained to visit neighboring residents, businesses, and institutions for conversation with them.

3. *Public documents.* A great deal of community contextual and environmental research is happening around congregations all the time. This research is undertaken by community and educational organiza-

tions. It is readily available but often not considered or addressed by religious organizations.

4. *Public forums.* There are external opportunities for congregational members and leaders to learn about the present realities of their community through participation in community forum settings.

5. *PERCEPT.* The PERCEPT organization has some of the most useful and pertinent data about congregational and local demographics. It provides a portrait of the local community, its composition, and particular dimensions of its "market." For Episcopal congregations, the basic information is available through the Episcopal Church website.

Awareness of the dynamics of congregational life and mission also are essential to congregational vitality. Congregational leaders need to employ frameworks and assessment tools to understand their congregational mission and dynamics more thoroughly. This chapter cannot begin to identify all of the frameworks or assessment resources, but it can identify a few of the most essential.

CONGREGATIONAL SIZE

One of the most important frameworks used to understand congregational dynamics is congregational size. This framework is a particular contribution of the former Congregational Development Director of the Episcopal Church and the first Director of the Seabury Institute, Arlin Rothauge, whose pamphlet *Sizing Up a Congregation for New Member Ministry*[13] has become a classic in the area of congregational dynamics. The size of a congregation influences everything from evangelism to opportunities for mission to leadership dynamics. Dr. Rothauge identifies four sizes for American congregations.

* *Family:* 50 worshipers (average Sunday attendance) or less

This size is aptly named, because the dynamics of these congregations are like those of a family. There is usually a matriarch or patriarch, and the congregation may include one or two actual blood-related families. The priest tends to function as a "chaplain," although there are also new modes of priestly/sacramental leadership through the total ministry modes of pastoral teams functioning in small congregations.

* *Pastoral:* 50 to 150 worshipers

The pastor is truly at the center of the dynamics of this size congregation. He or she is responsible for much of the programming, teaching, and direction. Congregants want to know their pastor and attribute much accountability to that person and role. The pastor is also a primary conduit for welcoming newcomers and for their incorporation into a community.

* *Program:* 150 to 350 worshipers

Programs dominate the dynamics of the life of this size congregation. People become part of its life through participation in one of these programs or small ministry/fellowship groups. Often there is multiple staff in these churches (especially at the larger end of the grouping). One of the most difficult points of growth in this size is encountered at the point of an average Sunday attendance of about two hundred.

* *Resource:* more than 350 worshipers

These congregations are the most complex in terms of organizational dynamics. There are more programs and groups, and often there are subsidiary institutions (schools, foundations, community organizations, and the like). They will usually have many human and financial resources for mission.

Congregational leaders can use this framework as a way of assessing the dynamics of their congregational life. It is absolutely necessary in defining the leadership and program offerings of a congregation and setting expectations about parish life. A great deal of work has been done on the transitional periods a congregation will experience as it moves from one size to another. These periods of transition are fraught with particular challenge and opportunity.

CONGREGATIONAL LIFE CYCLE

Arlin Rothauge has again provided the foundation for these findings through his presentation of the dynamics of congregational life cycle.[14] Using learnings about the human life cycle and studies of organizations, he describes the dimensions of birth, growth, development, stability, decline, and (sometimes) death for congregations.

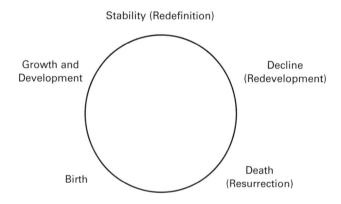

Stability (Redefinition)

Growth and Development

Decline (Redevelopment)

Birth

Death (Resurrection)

Every congregation is somewhere in its life cycle, as is every living organism. Two things are essential for congregational leaders in their mission direction. First, they must know where they are. When I am working with congregational leaders I invariably have them put an X on the place in the life cycle drawing where they believe they are, so that they can identify and have a conversation about the particular dynamics, challenges, and opportunities which face them at that given point. It is also helpful for leaders to know if they have a common vision about their congregation, or if there is a real difference of viewpoint among them.

The second thing that leaders must address is their responsibility to shape the future mission of the congregation and approach challenges and opportunities of life cycle in an intentional and planned way. Dr. Rothauge uses three R's to name the interventions offered by leaders: Redefinition, Redevelopment, and Resurrection. At the center of all three is essential reengagement with mission and the development of a vision and plan for congregational development, vitality, and renewal. Different strategies and a different intention are required with these three interventional responses, but mission awareness, articulation, and planning is of the essence to all of them.

CONGREGATIONAL ASSESSMENT
The assessment of congregational mission, context, attitudes, and dynamics is essential to everything we have described in this section. There are very useful forms and instruments of assessment currently available to congregational leaders, especially from the Episcopal Church Center, the Alban Institute, and the Gallup Organization.

The Episcopal Church Center's Congregational Development Unit offers information about average Sunday attendance, membership, and plate and pledge income for every Episcopal congregation and diocese. All clergy and vestries should be aware of this information for their own assessment, and should actually have the ten-year printout available for congregational leaders. In similar fashion, all bishops, standing committees, and diocesan councils should be aware of this information for Episcopal dioceses and their local congregations.

QUESTIONS FOR YOUR CONGREGATION

1. Are your congregational leaders aware of these frameworks and their importance for understanding a congregation's life and mission?

2. When did your congregation last do an assessment of its context and demographics? What did you learn?

3. How does the size of your congregation affect the way you do your mission and ministry?

4. Where is your congregation in its life cycle?

A CONGREGATION'S STORY

"The problem is that no one lives in this community anymore. You know that we all drive in from someplace else in order to go to this church." These were Jack's words at the St. Margaret's Church vestry meeting. In one sense, he was right. Ten of the dozen people sitting at that table did come from a distance to go to this congregation, with its average worship of 120 people on Sunday. However, the youngest member of the vestry said, "Well, that's true, Jack, but I have also recently discovered something else. I was surfing the website of the Episcopal Church head-quarters in New York, and found a link to this demo-graphic service called PERCEPT. It was fascinating. Did you know that there are actually a lot of new people in this neighborhood, living in the renovated and new buildings that all of us, except Lisa and Toni, pass on our way to church? The website said that we could get more extensive information about this. What do you all think?"

The vestry made the decision to pursue this idea further and did two things. It had one member contact the PERCEPT organization to get the full report, and it had the rector phone the diocesan office to talk with the congregational development officer. Both results were helpful and, in many ways, transforming for the congregation. The demographic data helped them to see that there were actually many new people and families in their community; somehow they had missed seeing them before. They began to focus on particular areas where they might offer these new neighbors an intentional invitation to come to St. Margaret's.

The diocesan congregational development officer was also extremely helpful to St. Margaret's and its leaders. Using the frameworks of congregational size and life cycle, she helped them to understand the particular methods of evangelism that would be most effective in a congregation their size. She also had them identify just where they were in their life cycle as a congregation. The primary "Aha!" moment in that reflection came when every vestry member put an X on exactly the same place in the life cycle diagram. They agreed the congregation was in steady decline, and had been for a whole decade. They learned what it would take to begin a process of congregational redevelopment and decided to use other resources and consultation available from the diocese for their work. "My eyes have been opened," said Jack. "I never saw our community or the life of this church in this way before."

There is a lot of work for St. Margaret's to do, and they are just beginning. However, the congregation's leadership believe that it is doable work, and they are committed to trying.

the learning congregation

Learning is one of the primary characteristics of vital and growing congregations. In his book *The Learning Congregation*, Thomas R. Hawkins presents the thesis that learning is *the* appropriate response from and focus of local communities of faith in the time of whitewater change. In response to present challenges, he believes, "We cannot manage our way out of the present crisis with better programs or more sophisticated marketing techniques. Developing a new consciousness of ourselves and our task requires generative learning." He goes on to describe the theological framework for this learning disposition and stance: "Stated theological learning involves conversion.... When we learn, we have a fundamental shift of the mind. Learning involves a transformation in our perspective, a change in the mental maps through which we make sense of reality."[15]

A spirit and disposition of education and formation identify the congregation and its life in vital communities of faith. Learning is developed for all ages according to the resources that are available to the congregation. Learning is essential to transformation of individuals and of a congregation. Learning areas include:

1. *Holy Scripture.* Encountering the narratives that undergird our faith and experience of God can include academic resources, but the type of formation that allows for a more life-based intersection with scripture is of critical importance.

2. *Episcopal identity.* Learning about who we are and the traditions that we share form people in the particular identity of this church, with its hopeful elements of respect, inquiry, openness, and scriptural authenticity.

3. *Mission.* Reflection on the present mission of God's church and the opportunities for service and transformation in the world is crucial.

4. *Personal call and vocation.* Opportunity should be given to individuals to explore their identity and their call to service and leadership in the church and world.

5. *Ministry in daily life.* The congregation should provide the means of learning and reflection on the experiences and meaning of daily living, particularly identifying the points of intersection between faith and daily experience.

6. *Context and culture.* Learning about what is really happening in the world around us, with particular attention to issues in our world, context, and culture, is essential.

7. *Spiritual practices.* Learning should introduce basic practices that inform and shape Christian life and belief.

8. *Marriage, commitment, and family learning.* Congregational learning should offer formation in the areas of human life and relationships that are at the center of the lives that people live day by day.

9. *Evangelism.* Teaching people how to tell their own faith stories and to become comfortable in their role of invitation to friends, co-workers, and family is part of learning within the congregation.

There has been substantial progress in the learning and formation experienced by local congregations in recent years. Children, young people, and adults have all benefitted from these new efforts and programs that enhance learning and transformation. Some examples include:

♦ *Godly Play and Catechesis of the Good Shepherd.*
Both of these Montessori-based programs have
contributed dramatically to the formation of children
and their love for and experience of the biblical story.
These are hands-on forms of learning where children
see and touch biblical images. My own children still
recall the power of the *Godly Play* stories they encountered as children in the parish where they grew up.

♦ *Journey to Adulthood.* This program of catechesis
for adolescents has gained wide use and a solid
reputation. It is a substantial investment of time in
learning—three years—as young people encounter
scripture, story, and learning to assist them in
forming their Christian identity. Important rites mark
significant transitional moments in the lives of participants. Adult mentoring, service, and pilgrimage are
parts of this program of youth transformation.

♦ *Education for Ministry (EFM) and Disciples of
Christ in Community (DOCC).* Both of these
programs are for adult learning, using an action/
reflection model that joins scripture and theology
with everyday living and experience. They build small
communities of learning, fellowship, and leadership
that contribute to the transformation of individuals
and congregations.

♦ *Alpha and Via Media.* These two programs of evangelism and identity help to form adults in faith. They
provide invitation and introduction to belief and
orientation to life in Christ and the church. They
involve intentional welcome and fellowship as an
integral part of the learning.

♦ *Groundwork I, II, and III.* This series was prepared for a combination of spiritual and scriptural reflection during the Lenten seasons in Years A, B, and C and learning and action planning for mission and evangelism. They can be used at any time of the year to help people grow more deeply into their own faith commitments and to invite others into their congregational life.

Each of these programs has strengths and weaknesses that make them appropriate for a particular congregation at a particular time. The important thing to remember when discerning which program to choose is that a congregation must set its sights on providing learning and formation opportunities for people of all ages. No single program will fit for everyone, and leaders in the congregation must ensure that there are many opportunities and possibilities for learning. Then formation becomes transformation for children and adults alike.

QUESTIONS FOR YOUR CONGREGATION

1. Have you done an inventory of Christian formation efforts available in your congregation? What are the strongest offerings? The weakest?

2. How do the children of your congregation find joy in their learning?

3. Are youth and young adults well served in their educational needs?

4. How are adults encouraged to go more deeply into their faith and formation?

A CONGREGATION'S STORY

The Church of the Holy Communion is a congregation experiencing a real renaissance—a renaissance brought about through learning. It is a growing congregation in a large urban area, a church that not too many years ago had been given up for dead. It was in serious decline to the point of having a total attendance of a couple of dozen people for Easter. Thought had been given to closing the congregation, but its first revitalization came as the parish engaged in committed actions of outreach and service in their local community. There were more people in church but very few children and young people.

That has changed. Holy Communion did its mission reflection and leadership work, engaged its renewing external community more effectively, and learned about the significant amount of new housing that was being built in that community. They decided to invest financial and human resources in learning, education, and formation. It began with a new look at Christian formation for children. The *Godly Play* formation approach was introduced with great results. Children actually brought their parents to church and to Sunday school, and the number of youngsters in the Christian education program quickly quadrupled. The congregation is now working to introduce *Journey to Adulthood* as a means of formation for their present cadre of youth and for this influx of young children when they arrive at their teenage years.

Adult formation and learning is also a part of the plan for congregational transformation through learning at Holy Communion. A new adult formation working group was commissioned. It had its first meeting and a very interesting conversation. It was discovered that one of the members had completed EFM (Education for Ministry) at another parish and knew that some people at Holy Communion were indicating interest in a group for the parish itself. They decided to work on that, and see where it would go. The good news is that it did go well, and a group now exists in the congregation.

The adult formation group has introduced various short-term studies and a long-term centering prayer opportunity for the congregation. Lenten and short-term Bible study offerings have been well received by the congregation. However, the working group wants to do more. They are now planning two short-term study groups that will be for parents with a focus on parenting and spiritual resources. People seem to be eager for the offering.

Learning is the foundation of the renewal and vitality being experienced in the Church of the Holy Communion. There is the realization that learning is transforming in and of itself. It allows people to explore new areas of their own faith and living. The congregation has also come to realize that focus on children and youth (and now young adults) and their learning is utterly essential to their vitality. The church has opened its doors to a preschool, which is introducing even more children and families to its congregation and its life. Some young parents and other parish members have also joined in a cooperative venture with other congregations to form an "urban" Episcopal School, a school that will serve children who are at risk but who could benefit greatly from this focus of learning.

Learning has translated into vitality for the Church of the Holy Communion. The clergy and lay leaders of the parish have seen people and their congregation transformed by the power of life-long learning. And at Easter last year seven hundred people of all ages showed up.

evangelism: plan and action

"Will you proclaim by word and example the Good News of God in Christ?" That is the question and promise posed about evangelism in the Book of Common Prayer's

Baptismal Covenant. The proclamation of Good News is at the very core of Christian mission and congregational life. We are called to present and proclaim God's love through Jesus Christ so that people may be invited into that love.

Earlier we saw that one of the primary characteristics of vital congregations identified in both the Faith Communities Today and the U.S. Congregational Life surveys is intentional evangelism planning and action. There is a problem, though. While the majority of congregations indicate a desire to grow, only a minority pursue the planning and action that are necessary to that growth. Episcopalians still remain reticent about evangelism, for a variety of reasons.

It is essential that we come to see the urgent call for evangelism in every congregation today. The first reason for that urgency is the gospel itself. The gospel is the good news of hope, peace, joy, strength, fulfillment, and transformation. God wants people to have this news, and those of us who are believers have a particular responsibility for and call to announce this good and joyful news.

The second reason for the urgency of evangelism is the particular moment in which we live. People are searching. They are hungry for meaning in this postmodern world. There is readiness for the proclamation of the news. But...we have not done so well. We are in a systemic decline as a denomination. We are an aging church that has had difficulty in inviting and retaining young people. This is true for our whole denomination, and it is equally true for a majority of our congregations.

What are we to do about this? How do we respond to this urgency as local communities of faith? The answer from the Book of Common Prayer once again: "Proclaim by word and example the Good News of God in Christ." The only way to respond to the urgency is to proclaim the gospel as individuals and as congregations. It is to plan and follow through on actions of invitation and incorporation.

Two basic things are necessary. The first is the willingness and ability of individuals to tell their own faith story and to have the confidence in that story to invite people to consider the message and life of the Christian faith. Individual faith journey stories and reflection provide a foundation for the planning and action of a congregation. Every congregation should have an evangelism committee (whatever the particular nomenclature may be for this important function) and develop a plan for the mission of evangelism. In turn, the vestry has oversight for this important mission action. The *Groundwork* series has provided recommendations for this vestry responsibility.

Particular attention needs to be given to four areas and dynamics of the process of evangelism in the local congregation.

1. INVITATION

The first stage of the action of evangelism is invitation. People are invited into the community of faith. There are many modes of invitation. The most important one is personal: people inviting people to the fellowship of faith. Familiarity and internal connection with one's own faith story contribute to the comfort level of believers to invite others to hear the Good News and to become part of the community of faith.

Daily life offers various possibilities for personal invitation. Conversations with other people, especially at times of transition or personal inquiry in the lives of those people, offer special opportunity. *Groundwork II* provides a training module for sharing faith through conversations. The promise of our Baptismal Covenant is to present the Good News "by word and example"; conversations are important, but so are the exemplary actions and witness of service, prayer, and compassion. What are the visible ways that you demonstrate your convictions and beliefs? Personal invitation is the strongest invitation, but there are many other modes of invitation that can be pursued by a congregation.

◆ *Advertising.* Parish advertising makes a difference. Radio and television advertising is more accessible to congregations than generally imagined. Good resources exist for congregational advertising plans using the media. *Groundwork I* gives examples. Print advertising is also useful for local congregations. One of the best modes are the small community newspapers that exist in towns and in large cities. Purchased advertising or prepared announcements and stories likewise yield a good result. Display advertising is also used by some congregations through billboards and signage on buses and subways.

◆ *Congregational websites, blogs, and podcasts.* Electronic communication is a newer world for most congregations, but learning how to use it is essential today. An attractive, inviting, and informative website is crucial for every congregation, especially if it wants to invite and attract young adults and youth into its midst. Other modes of electronic communication also offer invitational opportunities.

◆ *Special event evangelism.* Congregations offer all sorts of special events, such as concerts, lectures, social occasions, even pet blessings. Often they are considered parish events only, even though they are of interest to others outside the local congregation. Intentionally planning and using them for invitation offers a whole new level of evangelism potential.

◆ *Mailings, door hangers, postcards, and fliers.* Try the simple but effective use of target mailings (lists are available locally) and door hangers. The mailing strategy is more expensive but can be effective, if multiple mailings are used. Door hangers, postcards, and fliers are less expensive and can usually be produced with the talents of parishioners. *Groundwork III* provides examples.

✦ *Community gatherings and service occasions.* Special community events and gatherings are great occasions for invitations. Using some of the other tools described in this section, a congregation can have people and materials of invitation available at everything from the Lions Club fish fry to the charity marathon or walk.

✦ *Location, location, location.* One of the most invitational possibilities for a congregation is its own setting and location. However, the congregation has to think through how its site and facilities are invitational and how they are not. Signage is an often overlooked possibility

What can you think of? There are other possibilities for invitation in the life of congregations. What have you thought of? What are you pursuing? What might be done next?

2. WELCOME

The second stage of congregational evangelism is welcome. Most congregations of the Episcopal Church identify themselves as warm and welcoming, but what is lacking is the intentional strategy for welcome. Even the best intentions cannot replace plan and action for welcome.

Generally, congregations are more welcoming to people who fit the particular profile of the congregation as it exists in the present. More intentional welcome is required for groups that are not well represented.

Attention to the welcome offered to young adults, young families, people whose ethnic identity are not in the norm of a congregation, and others is necessary if a congregation is going to offer real welcome to new groups of people. The following questions may be helpful as a congregation considers its practice of welcoming newcomers.

+ *What do people see?* Is the facility welcoming? Adequate parking, good signage, and quality maintenance are all essential for the "welcoming look." Does the church actually look hopeful in its facilities and "open for business"?

+ *How are people greeted?* Or perhaps the question should be, "Are people greeted?" It is not enough to assume that people will feel welcome. Every congregation should have trained greeters who offer a welcome and initial introduction to the worship of the congregation.

+ *How are people helped?* Are people left to their own devices, or is there a helpful hand for their first worship or special occasion experience? It is important for visitors and newcomers to have assistance in their Sunday morning experience. People need help with the liturgy and worship. They need to be recognized, welcomed, and accompanied to the social/fellowship part of the occasion.

+ *Is there follow-up?* Newcomers and visitors need some kind of follow-up. The research demonstrates that the time elapsed from visit to follow-up makes a difference. The sooner the follow-up, the more likely a visitor is to return. An evangelism plan must include this important dimension.

+ *Is initial information about the congregation readily available?* Is there attractive information that describes the congregation and its mission? Does this information invite people to enter the life of the congregation more deeply?

♦ *Does your congregation effectively welcome people who differ from the "normal" group?* People who are outside the "normal" clientele of a congregation are often invisible—or worse, they are discouraged rather than encouraged to be part of the congregation. Congregational leaders need to be aware of this in reflecting on their congregation's welcome of younger people and others who are not part of the congregation's present characteristic group.

♦ *Are there welcoming occasions supported by the congregation?* A congregation needs to continue the welcoming process beyond the first experience. Newcomers' groups or events are essential to congregational evangelism. They are helpful occasions for informal and formal welcome.

3. INCORPORATION

Some congregations leave people at the welcome stage, with members believing that they have completed their evangelism tasks at that point. This is not the case. The real work and experience of transformation occur in the final two stages of the evangelism journey. People need to be invited into their further journey of transformation and into the congregation's life and experience of transformation.

How do people enter more deeply into the Christian faith and life? That is the question of the incorporation stage. "Incorporation" means literally "in the body" (from the Latin *in corpus*). This is the point where people enter the Body of Christ in a deep, lasting, and sustained way. Many traditional Christian spiritual practices are useful for the incorporation process. Similarly, several of the learning opportunities and programs describe previously in this chapter (Alpha, Via Media, Disciples of Christ in Community, and Education for Ministry) also offer opportunities for going more deeply into Christian belief and practice.

Some learning experiences are focused on people who are entering a congregation or the Christian faith for the first time. Two of them are of particular importance.

◆ *The Adult Catechumenate.* Based on the Roman Catholic Rites of Christian Initiation, this is intended primarily for adults who express interest in Holy Baptism. It is a program rooted in the practices of the ancient Christian church come alive for people preparing for this sacramental action in our own time.

◆ *Adult "Journey in Faith" programs.* Many of these programs are based on the catechumenal process but are not focused only on adults preparing for Holy Baptism. Rather, they are learning processes for adults who are examining their own faith and the covenant of their baptism. People for whom the Christian faith is completely a new experience, those who are entering a congregation from some other Christian community or tradition, and long-time church members who want to deepen their faith all benefit from this type of in-depth learning and prayer.

Other learning groups may be used for this incorporation purpose too. The important thing is that the evangelism process points to this deepening experience and intentionally connects people to these programs and opportunities.

4. SENDING

The Christian faith is "apostolic" in its very essence, which means that it sends people for mission. The last stage of the evangelism process is sending people into their own ministry, mission, and service. Some people discover their own sense of call in mission. Others require a more focused and intentional structure than is generally available at this time.

It is important for the congregation to find ways of assisting people to discover more about their own sense of call and purpose. Sam Portaro's volume on vocation in this *Transformations* series will assist people in the process of discernment. In addition, four other resources for vocational discernment are of particular use at this time:

♦ *Listening Hearts.* This personal discernment program helps people to listen to their own hearts and to what God may be saying to them. Its purpose is to help people in decisions and discernment about their own particular call and service.

♦ *The Gallup "Living Your Strengths" Program.* This assessment book and instrument helps people to discern their particular strengths, styles, and enthusiasms. It makes a direct connection to the type of service and sending that might be most appropriate for individuals.

♦ *Parker Palmer's* A Hidden Wholeness. This method, rooted in the Quaker tradition, assists people in their vocational search in several ways. One of the most useful is the "clearness committee," a form of communal discernment that helps people to make decisions about their lives, call, opportunities, and potential service.

♦ *Richard Boyatzis and Anne McKee's* Resonant Leadership. Yes, it's a book on leadership, but it has several tools that can be used by any individual to gain more focus on personal call and service.

A congregation can also use other means for the sending stage of the evangelism process. Stewardship programs that emphasize the giving of talent and personal gifts for ministry are effective in the stage. Every congregation should have a clear and up-to-date listing of service ministries that are available through the life of that community of faith.

1. Who is responsible for the ministry of evangelism in your own congregation?

2. What are the strengths that your congregation has for inviting, welcoming, incorporating, and sending?

3. What are the barriers to effective evangelism in your congregation?

4. What are the steps you can take to enhance the mission of evangelism?

5. Does your congregation have a plan for evangelism? What actions have been taken to implement the plan? Who is in charge? How is effectiveness evaluated?

A CONGREGATION'S STORY

The mountainous area around St. Paul's Episcopal Church is lovely, and the town itself is historic and gracious. St. Paul's has been essentially the same size congregation for several generations, blessed with people who love it and the Lord it serves. Both the town and the congregation have long viewed themselves as quintessential small town America, but things are changing.

The town itself is changing rapidly. A new freeway was completed, and the major city that was once three hours away is now accessible in half the time. The result has been a steady development of new housing communities around the town. People are moving in, and both the town and St. Paul's Episcopal Church need to make some response.

The rector and local congregation chose to spend their recent Lenten study using the *Groundwork* series offered by the Episcopal Church to focus on the meaning of and opportunity for evangelism. They had to do some internal work. The congregation has always prided itself on being a "friendly" church full of welcome and warmth. However, they had to be honest that it was easier to do this for each other, as small town folk, rather than for new unknown suburbanites. They considered this and came to a decision: the gospel requires real invitation and the action of evangelism.

They put some of the suggestions of the *Groundwork* series to work. They did a "walk about" of their facilities to see if they were really as welcoming as they purported to be (and even refurbished the parish nursery, horrified to see what they had taken for granted). They developed a door-hanger project, producing a packet of materials and a clear statement of welcome that they delivered to the front doors of the neighborhood. For years they had made the best desserts available at the two town festivals; now they had materials and people available to introduce the church to many newcomers to the community. They offered a pet blessing for the whole town, and it seemed the whole town showed up.

The rector and small evangelism committee have envisioned some further goals for their evangelism efforts. They have trained greeters and created both a "user friendly" coffee hour program and a bread delivery system for newcomers. Now they are working on ways to introduce their church and incorporate the growing number of visitors to their congregation, a congregation that is rapidly growing. It's good news all around.

Communities of
Transformation

In this chapter we continue to look in turn at a number of the marks of vital and effective congregations— communities of faith that are places of transformation—this time focusing more specifically on the life and worship of the congregation. Here we consider the importance of worship and preaching that is engaging and focused on congregational mission; leadership development, both lay and ordained; dealing directly with conflict; the creation of a hopeful climate and flexibility toward change; the experience of a caring community; opportunities for compassionate service; and stewardship of resources.

transformational worship
and preaching

Worship and preaching are essential to congregational vitality. They are at the center of the primary gatherings of regular attenders and newcomers. There are many styles, theological emphases, and traditions that can be employed. In every instance worship and preaching must be compelling, hopeful, and inviting.

Worship and preaching must serve as means for transformation. They bear and reflect the transforming love and power of God. They engage the human heart, mind, and soul in a way that connects them to God. When the primary statements about deepening relationship with God and connecting closely to God occur in the Faith Communities Today survey, they are related quite clearly to worship and preaching. These two Christian practices form and shape human relationship with God and forge a deeper connection and communication with God.

WORSHIP

How does worship transform human beings? Ritual actions, words, symbols, songs, and prayer are expressions of transformation in worship. Christians have been worshiping God and experiencing transformation through prayer for two thousand years. A rich tradition of prayer undergirds present Christian worship. However, there are also many contemporary modes of worship that enliven the heart and enrich the soul.

The Faith Communities Today survey and U.S. Congregational Life Survey identify two primary attributes that are important to our understanding of worship and the vitality of congregational life: joy and transcendence. Christian worship needs to be joyful, not turgid or dreary. At the same time, it needs to be transcendent in its nature, transporting the Christian worshiper into the mystery of God. It cannot be pedestrian or sloppy.

Some resources for worship that enhance its joyful and transcendent characteristics include the following:

◆ *New forms of public prayer.* Most congregations of the Episcopal Church continue to use the 1979 Book of Common Prayer. It has various forms for worship, but it in no way exhausts the possibilities for joyful worship. *Enriching Our Worship* is a very useful resource, for example, offering worship with more inclusive language. Other forms of public prayer are also available today. Many congregations are employing prayer from other Anglican prayer books and orders of worship from other denominations and religious communities. The Emerging Church movement is also producing patterns of prayer that can be translated from one congregational setting to another.

✦ *New forms of music.* Both the Iona and Taizé communities offer forms of music that are both joyful and transcendent. Other musical resources are available from denominational and nondenominational sources. The musical life of the Episcopal Church is deeply enriched by the publication of *Lift Every Voice and Sing II, El Himnario, Wonder, Love, and Praise,* and *Voices Found.* Other compilations of hymns, songs, and praise music can enrich the musical experience of a congregation. Instrumentation is no longer limited to the organ—piano, guitar, and all manner of other instruments may be employed to offer praise and worship to God.

✦ *Learning about transforming worship.* Congregations can learn about new possibilities for worship through websites and gatherings that are devoted to worship and its practice.

One style of worship is not necessarily preferable to another. In fact, many growing congregations use different styles of worship reflecting the different interests and needs of members and potential members. The style of worship is not the issue (although many Episcopal congregations get stuck and stymied on this point). The question is, How is worship experienced? Is it joyful? Does it provide meaning and hope? Is there a sense of the transcendence and mystery of the divine within it? Does it bring people closer to God? These are the worship questions for your congregation.

PREACHING

Now here's a tough issue. One of the marks and characteristics of vital congregations is good and hopeful preaching. In fact, preaching is critical to congregational vitality. In the study of effective Episcopal clergy undertaken by John Dreibelbis and David Gortner, one of the striking discoveries was that the identification of good preaching among effective clergy actually correlated with the numerical growth of the congregation.

As with worship, there are many styles of preaching, but there are four essential descriptors of preaching connected to congregational vitality.

♦ *It is biblical.* The Bible is used as a foundation for preaching but not in a dogmatic way. Rather, its power of narrative, metaphor, poetry, and song is employed for the purposes of transformation. Good, postmodern preaching is as evocative as *Godly Play* for children in its approach to Holy Scripture.

♦ *It is joyful.* This does not mean that it is unrealistic or naïve about the human condition and sinfulness. Joyful preaching means that its heart and center is the proclamation of hope. The gospel is the good news of new life, new hope, and new meaning for people, and it needs to be proclaimed as such.

♦ *It is life-related.* The days of expository preaching are dead and gone. Preaching today must be life-related. It weaves a hopeful connection between God's love and human daily existence. It connects to the themes, concerns, and issues of modern and even postmodern living.

♦ *It is invitational.* All preaching should be evangelical to some degree. It is the proclamation of Good News in a way that people are invited into closer relationship with God. It also invites them into the life and fellowship of a local community of faith.

QUESTIONS FOR YOUR CONGREGATION

1. How would you characterize the worship and preaching of your congregation? Do they have life? Is there an attitude of joy and hopefulness?

2. What are the comments that visitors and newcomers make about your worship and preaching? Do people seem refreshed by the experience? Is God's love palpable?

3. What range of worship and music resources, ideas and materials do you use?

4. What do congregational members value most about your church's worship and preaching?

A CONGREGATION'S STORY

They actually thought it was time to close the Church of the Ascension, and a priest had been sent there to do just that. The few remaining elderly people could be cared for until there were none left, and the property could be maintained well enough until it would be sold. This was going to be a peaceful transition, and there was no animosity between the congregation and the diocese.

Now a decade later, Ascension Church is still open. In fact, it averages some 300 worshipers each week in its city setting. It's a wonderful community of faith—hopeful, diverse, and full of energy. What happened? Several things, but primary among them was interaction with the surrounding community through joyful worship and hopeful preaching.

The worship and preaching are delightful at the Ascension. The worship reflects many sources, including the Book of Common Prayer, contemporary worship communities, other Anglican and Christian books and resources, new Episcopal resources, and the congregation's own compositions. Careful planning helps to integrate these abundant resources for prayer, just as it does with music. The Episcopal *Hymnal 1982* is used along with several other musical sources. The instrumentation includes organ, piano, guitar, and flute in a traditional and innovative style, and the nearby city school for folk music does at least a couple appearances there each year.

When parish members describe the worship of Ascension Church, they highlight two aspects: the sense of joy and openness in their prayer and music, and the hopeful and invitational preaching of their priest. Church is often surprising but seldom boring. The worship itself is most often depicted as being zesty and celebrative. The priest preaches sermons that are both hopeful and challenging. The preaching is scriptural and life-related at the same time, and always there is a twofold invitation to go deeper into one's own faith and to enter the community of the parish more fully. The message: God loves you and welcomes everyone into a deeper experience of that love. And... the message is heard.

The Church of the Ascension knows that worship and preaching transform people in their believing and living. The clergy and leaders work hard to keep their worship fresh. The priest, and an increasing number of lay preachers and student assistants, continue to focus on and learn about the communication of the gospel, and they try new as well as tried-and-true methods. Through worship, music, and preaching, newcomers know that God has invited them here, and they heed the invitation.

lay and clergy leadership development

Mission requires leadership. Vital congregations require good leaders, both lay and ordained, and give attention to the support and ongoing development of their leaders.

ORDAINED LEADERS

Clergy are not fully developed in their leadership the moment they graduate from seminary. Much more is required, and, in many ways, the seminary educational experience does not build leadership capacities adequately. In his study of pastoral excellence, the eminent leadership and congregational life researcher Jackson Carroll suggests several areas of excellence and responsibility for congregational ministers. He defines "good pastoral leadership" as "the process of helping a congregation embody in its corporate life the practices that shape vital Christian life and community in ways that are faithful to the Gospel and appropriate to the particular congregation's size, resources, and setting—especially its existence in 21st century American society." Carroll then suggests the following tasks:

  ♦ Teaching a congregation about the meaning of practices that shape vital and faithful Christian life and community—that is, an interpretive task;

  ♦ Helping a congregation gain a critical understanding of its current practices, resources, and setting—that is, a social-analytical task;

  ♦ Helping a congregation gain a vision of itself as a vital Christian community that is realistic given its size and resources and setting—that is, an envisioning task;

* Motivating a congregation's members to pursue its vision by shaping its practices in keeping with the vision—that is, a motivational and "incarnational" task;

* Helping the congregation find the resources—spiritual, intellectual, and material—to pursue the vision and maintain its life—that is, resource development task;

* Coping with and managing the inevitable conflicts that come from multiple constituencies and points of view in the congregation—that is, a political task;

* Monitoring the congregation's life and practices so that they retain their faithfulness to the gospel in light of ever-changing reality—that is, a task of ongoing renewal.

Carroll concludes that "these tasks will be carried out differently in different congregations, taking into account the congregation's denominational tradition, history, size and context, but taken together, they constitute the practice of good pastoral leadership."[16]

John Dreibelbis and David Gortner have pursued similar reflections through research into the qualities and characteristics of effective Episcopal clergy leaders. They have found that effective leadership is "confident, clear, creative, collaborative and consistent." These leaders emphasize the proclamation of the gospel and have an evangelistic perspective. (They are also good preachers.) They build relationships for mission and utilize the faith tradition in a vital and "living" way.

According to Dreibelbis and Gortner, mentors and mentorship have been key developing forces for effective leaders. The leaders themselves are mission-focused (even to the point of having a higher level of focus on mission in the search and interview connections with prospective new parishes). They know how to build partnerships and networks and how to "get things done." Effective clergy leaders reflect hope and enthusiasm for their work and for the mission of the church. They understand their context and environment, and they overcome the "natural" clergy aversion to and avoidance of conflict, working to negotiate and resolve conflict when it occurs.[17]

The Faith Communities Today survey identified five attributes that best described an Episcopal clergyperson as someone who cares about people, is an effective worship leader, good liturgist, and hard worker, and who knows the Bible. These are good things, to be sure. However, the five characteristics that least describe Episcopal clergy are more troubling. They are: charismatic leader (the very lowest rated), evangelistic, effective administrator, someone who knows how to get people to work together, and someone who knows how to get things done. These are leadership characteristics and attributes that must be developed if we are to be more effective leaders and a more effective church.

LAY LEADERS

The development of lay leadership is also essential to mission development and congregational progress. Even more important, leadership development among lay people contributes to their sense of vocation and purpose, thereby having a positive effect on their own lives, the life of the church, and ministry in the world.

The problem is that congregations (like most dioceses, seminaries, and other church organizations) do not do enough to enhance the leadership of their lay members. Lay leadership still remains a largely untapped and undeveloped resource for the mission of God's church. However, for those congregations that develop the leadership of lay members, the result is positive and hopeful. Two areas of leadership in particular greatly enhance the mission vitality and development of a congregation: personal leadership and group leadership.

Personal leadership
The development of lay leadership requires a process and program that will assist people to learn and experience more about their own call and identity as leaders. It will assist them to do the "inner work" of leadership (both lay and ordained). Here are five focus areas of "inner work" that enhance the capacity and practice of leaders. They are related to the areas of "emotional intelligence" that are so important to positive, hopeful, and effective leadership.

1. *Reflection.* This is the capacity to examine and appraise one's own personal history, call, and behavior. An essential dimension of leadership inner work is the internal reflection on life history and the decisions, events, and people that have shaped the journey of the leader. The leader also reflects on his or her own call and purpose and the behaviors that forward that call, as well as the behaviors that inhibit it.

2. *Framework.* Leaders strategically identify strengths and hopes in their lives and the organizations they serve. They frame this identification in realistic and optimistic ways, and interpret negative events and challenges with inner strength, narrative, and response. They develop the gift and capacity of resilience (a gift and capacity especially important for congregational and religious leaders).

3. *Attunement.* Values and actions of life are attuned and congruent. They examine their values and actions and seek to learn from others. In so doing they "talk the talk and walk the walk."

4. *Conviction.* There is a sense of capacity and conviction in the practice of leadership. The leaders do the

inner work to understand one's own convictions and sense of truth. They then trust, value, and speak from that understanding.

5. *Replenishment.* Life and leadership can be very challenging for people. This dimension of the inner work involves the craft of "counterpoint." This is the ability to restore perspective and renew resources for the work of leadership.[18]

Leaders must do their own personal and inner work to sustain their practice of leadership and to build their own capacities. Such leaders are essential congregational mission and development.

Group leadership
Attention must also be given to the development of groups of leaders in congregational life, especially the church governing board (vestry, bishop's committee, chapter). Again, this is done quite sporadically in Episcopal congregations. So many church governing board members attend to their monthly meetings but do nothing more. As such, their capacity of leadership is not developed in a full way.

Elements that are necessary to leadership development of governing boards include the following:

+ *Time apart.* This simply cannot be done in a monthly meeting. Boards need to have time apart to focus on the deeper and broader issues of congregational life and mission.

+ *Good facilitation.* Intentional and capable facilitation of this group in leadership education is essential. It can be done by the resident clergyperson, if that individual is trained in this work. Preferably it is done by external facilitation and consultation.

♦ *Relationship to other groups of leaders.* Participation in leadership education with other leaders in the congregation and outside the local community of faith helps build local capacity. Many dioceses are introducing vestry/wardens conferences.

♦ *Mission-focused learning.* The governing board of a local congregation must focus on the substantive questions of mission. They are responsible for the mission of the congregation and must offer that leadership.

♦ *Vision and planning for the future.* Again, the governing board is the unit responsible for future vision and planning. Part of its leadership education is in the area of planning.

Richard Chait has listed the following dimensions as essential to the leadership education and functioning of a board or other group of leaders:

♦ *Contextual dimension.* The board understands the institution's mission, tradition and history, making sure that the board's behaviors are consistent with institutional values.

♦ *Educational dimension.* The board emphasizes the need to learn to seek feedback on board performance and to provide opportunities for trustee education and self-reflection.

♦ *Interpersonal dimension.* The board nurtures the development of the trustees as a group, establishes group goals and consciously attends to the board's collective strength and welfare.

♦ *Intellectual dimension.* The board recognizes complexities, tolerates ambiguities, sees trustees as one constituency among many, and understands how different issues, actions, and decisions affect one another.

♦ *Political dimension.* The board respects and guards the integrity of the governance process, avoids win/lose situations, and accepts as one of its primary responsibilities the need to build healthy relationships among key constituencies.

♦ *Strategic dimension.* The board directs its attention to a few priorities or decisions identified as having strategic or symbolic importance to the institution.[19]

These are extremely important dimensions for any board and the leadership they exercise. Congregational board life does not just happen. It needs to be shaped and nurtured in each of the dimensions. I would add three other theology-based dimensions that I believe are particularly significant for the boards of Christian congregations:

♦ *Faith dimension.* The board believes that it is called and empowered by God for its work, takes time for prayer and reflection, and sees its work as part of a broader tradition of faith.

♦ *Hope dimension.* The board acknowledges that the future does belong to God and that it is preparing for that future; a realistic optimism is reflected in its members' attitude for their work.

♦ *Love dimension.* The board draws upon the love of God and shows charity to each other. Conflicts are named and steps are taken to address them. Forgiveness is a real dynamic in the leadership of the congregational board.

1. Does your congregation offer opportunities for individual leadership reflection and development?

2. Does your governing leadership group take time away for leadership development, mission articulation, and planning?

3. Do you know about and relate to other external modes of leadership education that are offered by local organizations or your own diocese?

A CONGREGATION'S STORY

Christ Church is one of the largest churches in the denomination. It has grown a great deal in recent years and has a wide variety of programs in which it takes great pride. Many resources exist at Christ Church, and the congregation has worked diligently to develop them. But a few years ago, they came to an important realization: they needed to develop the *human* resources of the congregation more fully. Out of that realization they developed a threefold plan for leadership development. The three elements were of the plan were:

1. A broad educational offering on leadership for any in the congregation who might have interest.

2. A retreat for congregational leaders to focus on leadership and congregational life.

3. A vestry education process.

All three elements yielded good effects for the congregation. The broad educational event was well attended by numerous people in the parish, and it led to further learning, conversation, and inquiry about the nature of leadership. The Christ Church Leaders' Retreat shaped long-time leaders and a new generation of emerging leaders, allowing them to meet and learn together for the first time. The event built community among them all and gave useful information to these new and continuing leaders. The vestry education process changed the way the vestry did its work and led to the initiation of a strategic planning process for the congregation.

By the time Christ Church had engaged so substantially in a leadership focus and development set of processes, it saw the positive effects on congregational life. Leaders were more aware of their own call and capacities for leadership and felt that they were part of a learning conversation about leadership. The parish's vestry and other committees were more intentional in their leadership, and there was a great alliance in leadership between clergy and lay leaders.

One lay leader was asked about the benefits of this work, and he responded, "We learned more about our call to be leaders and the nature of leadership in the church. This led to concrete action for stronger mission in this congregation and to a greater sense of leadership both inside the church and in the wider community." When asked if this could work only in a large congregation, she said, "Absolutely not. This focus on leadership is important to any congregation, and we are using it in the small seasonal congregation where my husband and I spend part of our time as a couple."

dealing directly with conflict

The data on conflict was quite clear in the 2005 Faith Communities Today survey: 93 percent of Episcopal congregations noted that they had experienced conflict at some point within the past five years. (I sometimes joke in teaching settings that this proves that only 7 percent of Episcopal congregations were predisposed to lie about this!) Conflict could be passing, or it could be enduring and debilitating. The two primary areas generating conflict were congregational finances and clergy leadership style. (In 2005 conflict was also identified around issues of human sexuality and biblical authority in the Episcopal Church.)

The question is not, "Will there be conflict?" Rather, the question is, "How do we negotiate and resolve conflict?" The first chapters of this book clearly name the change and transitions that all of us face in our lives, organizations, and congregations. Often the result is conflict in a time of such massive change.

One of the marks and characteristics of congregational vitality and growth is the willingness to deal directly with conflict. Denial and avoidance are not acceptable modes for these congregations. Conflict is not allowed to fester. Here are some ways to assess and respond to conflict in your congregation.

1. *Open and honest assessment.* Part of the work of leadership is to assess the pulse and climate of a community of faith. This can be done informally or through a process of surveying a local congregation. *Note:* If you do a congregational survey, plan on hearing some negative critique, and do not let it throw you in your leadership.

2. *Disciplined conversation around matters of disagreement.* Have focused and disciplined conversation about matters of disagreement. Doing this early on can keep conflict from escalating into more divisive issues.

3. *Have agreed-upon norms for conversation.* Before approaching issues of conflict and disagreement, have agreed-upon norms for conversation that encourage and embody respect, honesty, and safety for participants.

4. *Read something about conflict.* Good resources for understanding conflict and negotiation exist. Two of the best are the work of Speed Leas on conflict, published by the Alban Institute, and "Getting to Yes" by Roger Fisher and his colleagues at the Harvard Negotiation Project.

5. *Use external consultation as appropriate.* Congregations often wait until it is too late to utilize external consultation for conflict negotiation and resolution. Consultation is useful at various points along the way. The consultation can be about related issues of dialogue, norms, and communication before there is a more serious conflict.

Conflict does and always will exist in congregational life. Growing and vital congregations negotiate and deal with conflict. They also develop the norms and modes of communication that assist them in their mission and relationships in an ongoing way.

QUESTIONS FOR YOUR CONGREGATION

1. What are issues of disagreement in your congregation?

2. How are such issues addressed normally?

3. Are there new patterns of negotiation and dialogue that might be used to enhance congregational communication about difficult issues?

4. Have you ever used external resources to assist in conflict management and negotiation?

A CONGREGATION'S STORY
"How can there be such difficulty in a church where there are so many possibilities?" said one priest to another at a clergy gathering. "I don't know how, but I do know that it

has been going on for the better part of the last twenty years." It was true. There was a tradition of conflict in this congregation. It showed itself in the lay leadership, in the climate of the congregation, and in the clergy. The succession of rectors of St. Elizabeth's Church included one who died immediately after retirement, one who left the church after a brief tenure, one who left amid rumors of misconduct, and one who was fired. Yes, it was twenty years of conflict, and then some.

The issues of the conflict were numerous. Some were the big ones that confronted the wider Episcopal Church: a new Prayer Book, women's ordination, and human sexuality. Others were specific to St. Elizabeth's: how to use financial resources, leadership disagreements, and just plain mistrust. People didn't want to work together, and conflict dominated many gatherings and meetings.

The time of transformation came after the termination of a rector. The parish leadership realized that they simply could not call another person into the midst of the congregation with such a climate and tradition of anger. So, they set to work. They utilized external consultation with the vestry and search committee in a variety of ways. Some consultation presented norms and mechanisms to allow for communication and the building of trust. There was also consultation on the nature of effective ordained and lay ministry and what would be necessary for them to become a congregation focusing on mission rather than disagreements. The parish leadership agreed that they would not call a new rector until they had some consensus about the congregation's mission and the characteristics they actually sought in an ordained leader.

There is a new rector at St. Elizabeth's now, an ordained leader who is attuned to communication and conflict. It is not the case that there will never be conflict in that congregation again. There will be, and there is at present. But what has changed is the way that disagreements are addressed. Conversation and dialogue have replaced denial and accusation. There are regular open conversation opportunities with the rector, and the vestry has begun a system of intentional conversations with people throughout the parish. If an issue presents itself, the parish leadership talks about it without leaping to conclusions, using a discipline they have learned in which they can examine interests and options.

St. Elizabeth's is now a much healthier and happier congregation. Conflict no longer saps the strength of the congregation. Mutuality and dialogue are transforming the culture and climate of the congregation, and people are working together.

---

hopeful climate and flexible attitude

What is the climate of your congregation and its life? How do leaders and other people deal with change and challenge in congregational mission and experience? Growing and vital congregations are marked by a hopeful climate and flexible attitudes. This does not mean that these congregations are unrealistic and delusional in their perspectives. Rather, it means that these are congregations that realize and live out the hope that is inherent in the gospel and that they meet opportunities and challenges with resilience and flexibility.

One of the most hopeful approaches to organizational life in recent years has been Appreciative Inquiry, a discipline and approach of organizational assessment and planning that starts with the strengths and assets of an organization. It recognizes that these hopeful attributes do exist in organizational life and it intentionally begins with developing an awareness and analysis of them rather than with organizational problems and shortcomings. The result is planning that builds on strengths rather than weaknesses.

A hopeful climate is even broader than this approach to organizational assessment and planning, though. Climate is the environment and ambience of a congregation's life. Everything from Holy Scripture (remembering that God looked at his creation and called it "good") to the discipline of Appreciative Inquiry to the Harvard Business School study on hopeful versus pessimistic organizations emphasize the importance of hope, affirmation, and flexibility in organizational life. A hopeful approach goes a long way to accomplishing goals. A hopeful climate goes a long way in welcoming people and building the souls of congregational members. A hopeful and flexible attitude goes a long way in developing mission and meeting challenges.

QUESTIONS FOR YOUR CONGREGATION

1. Is a hopeful message proclaimed in worship, preaching, and community life?

2. Do newcomers describe their initial experience as one of hope and joy (or conversely as one of anxiety and even anger)?

3. Is there more conversation within your parish about possibilities for mission than problems and challenges?

4. Does your congregation tolerate or even seek opportunity and risk for the gospel?

5. Is your leadership willing to try new things?

6. Do you often hear statements like "We tried that before, and it didn't work" or "We just don't do things that way"?

7. Do people talk about being "stuck" and not able to move into new areas of mission?

A tiny congregation on the edge financially and in so many other ways—that was how a visitor perceived the Church of the Resurrection a few years ago. It was small: twenty or thirty people on good days in the midst of the summer when seasonal residents joined the stalwarts. For years the congregation tried to piece together clergy leadership by yoking with another congregation quite some distance away. The character of the two yoked congregations and their communities could not have been more different.

The congregation struggled. Its climate was fairly depressed, even though the people themselves were welcoming and caring. Clergy came and went, and some of them openly expressed their dislike for the setting and their hopelessness for the congregation. There certainly was very little hope in the air.

Then things began to change. A new priest arrived who was not full-time but would serve at the Church of the Resurrection only. She was well trained in congregational development and saw herself as a priest developer as well as a pastor. The community was also beginning to change. There were more year-round residents and a growing base of communities in the area.

More important, the Church of the Resurrection began to change. Both the new vicar and the lay leadership expressed and embraced hope. Visitors and newcomers experienced real invitation and had the impression that something significant and hopeful was happening in this local congregation. The vicar gave attention to the worship and preached sermons of invitation and hope. Christian formation offerings for children and adults were introduced, and the congregation launched small but regular community service and outreach activities.

A hopeful climate and flexibility in their approach and attitude became marks of this congregation. They entered more fully into scripture and into the good news of the gospel itself. Parish worship and gatherings reflected community and real joy. The congregation decided to operate out of its hope and has even envisioned a building project and the necessary capital funds drive to support it.

Things do change, and hope does emerge. The congregation and its leaders have done their work to reframe the way they view things, and they seldom say "We're just a tiny, struggling place" or "We would never have the resources to do that" anymore. This community of faith is on a journey together, a journey of hope and new beginnings.

caring community

One of the most ancient hymns of the Christian community is *Ubi caritas et amor, Deus ibi est* ("Where there is charity and love, God will be there too"). Charity, care, and love are essential marks of the Christian faith and community throughout the ages. They are also marks of growing and vital Christian communities in the present.

People are sustained, nurtured, and strengthened through caring community in a congregation. Most Episcopal congregations identify themselves as "warm and caring." That is good—though sometimes this applies primarily to the people who are already part of a community. Newcomers do not necessarily experience it. In the Faith Communities Today survey, there was a correlation between small congregations that identified themselves as "family" and an actual decline in membership. These congregations quite probably are very warm and caring within their existing relationships but they do not actively invite or welcome new people into that caring community. Here are some ways that growing and vital congregations are enhancing their caring ministries.

♦ *Caring is not just the work of clergy.* Yes, clergy are pastors and responsible for leadership of caring in the congregation. However, caring and pastoral work are not the domain of the clergy only. The caring ministry needs to be shared between clergy and laity.

♦ *There are many groups and relationships for caring.* The size of a congregation does not matter when it comes to caring community. In fact, members of many large congregations identify caring community as one of the attractive dimensions of congregational life. What does matter is the intentional grouping and relationships for caring.

♦ *People are noticed.* Caring congregations know their people and notice the changes and transitions in their lives.

♦ *There are structures and programs for caring.* Caring is not left to chance. A plan for caring ministry is prepared and enacted by a congregation. This may involve programs like Stephen Ministries or Parish Health Ministry. It may be less formal, but it is planned.

In our present American culture, there are far too few opportunities for caring. Many of us do not live in small towns or intimate environments. Mobility is the norm with people living in several different places over the course of a lifetime. Congregations bear an unusual and precious responsibility and possibility for caring. This caring enriches people's lives and strengthens them for daily living.

1. What are the primary modes of pastoral caring and ministry exhibited in your congregation?

2. Who assumes responsibility for caring and pastoral response?

3. Does your congregation have a healing ministry?

4. How might you increase pastoral caring and concern in your congregation?

A CONGREGATION'S STORY

It is a beautiful part of the world, with its trees, water, streams, rolling hills. St. Alban's Church had been there for well over a hundred years, a place where miners and mine owners worshiped together. People were proud of their heritage and of a long tradition of caring in the congregation. Most members can still tell the stories of the caring pastors that they had, but they can also tell you that it's been a long time since they had a pastor, full-time or even part-time. "You just can't have the same kind of caring pastoral presence with supply clergy, and to tell you the truth, they're pretty few and far between these days anyway," said the senior warden.

St. Alban's was facing the challenge that so many small congregations face today: how to have the pastoral care that they need and want to offer within their community of faith. They were still operating out of the assumption that pastoral care depended on a pastor's presence, even though they experienced great caring from one another, especially at times of crisis and transition.

St. Alban's senior warden expressed this frustration to the bishop during her annual visitation. The bishop replied, "You know, Sam, the traditional model is not the only way of having good pastoral care in a congregation. In fact, pastoral responsibility belongs to the whole congregation. Have you heard that we are beginning a new process of education in our diocese for ministry teams to offer pastoral care and leadership? The basic belief is that a congregation has the gifts and resources within it to do the ministry it is called to do. Would you be interested in learning more about this and its possibilities for St. Alban's?" Sam said, "Yes," and that's where the adventure began.

Discernment began within the congregation about the meaning of baptism, ministry, and mission. A few people expressed interest and were identified as those with the gifts to offer leadership as a part of a ministry team. St. Alban's utilized the ministry development learning process offered by the diocese, and the congregation was surprised by the results. A ministry team did emerge that fulfilled the sacramental, pastoral, educational, and missional needs of that small community of faith.

Pastoral care has now been transformed at St. Alban's. The reservoir of pastoral care has been replenished, and there is the realization that this care belongs to the whole congregation. Susan is the pastoral care coordinator, and she has developed a system of care within the congregation. Now they are working on a hospice care program for the whole community.

compassionate service

One of the greatest gifts given to the Christian community is compassion. This gift reflects the compassion of Christ himself, compassion shown throughout his ministry and in the supreme event of that ministry, his death on the cross. "Jesus, Thou art pure compassion," as the well-known hymn puts it. Jesus is compassion, and so are we.

Compassion is a sign of vital congregational life. Strong, growing congregations give visible action to their compassion through service, especially service to the external community. Creative congregations find the means of serving those who are in need in their community. There are some wonderful and noble stories of compassionate ministries of service to the hungry and homeless, of tutoring, housing, and community development programs, of volunteer service ministries—the list could go on.

Compassionate service is undertaken by vital congregations. They possess a vision of the sovereign love of God and the servanthood of Jesus Christ. One of the growing edges of this service is to see and depict it as a ministry of advocacy. While many congregations name their ministries as "compassionate service" in the Faith Communities Today survey, "advocacy" was rated last out of twelve possible descriptive congregational characteristics. There is a disconnect here. Congregations do compassionate service, but they do not seem to perceive this service as advocacy ministry for justice and the transformation of society.

Useful resources are available to local congregations for their ministries of compassionate service and advocacy. These include:

+ *Jubilee Ministries.* Ministries of compassion throughout the country find community and information through the Jubilee Ministries program of the Episcopal Church. Information is available on the Episcopal Church website.

+ *Prison ministries.* As is the case with Jubilee Ministries, information about networks and the practice of prison ministries is available from the Episcopal Church Center through its website.

✦ *Episcopal Community Services of America.* Many metropolitan areas benefit from ministries of compassion implemented by Episcopal Community Services. Recently a national organization of these ministries has formed.

✦ *Episcopal Peace Fellowship.* This long-standing national organization advocates for peace and reconciliation ministries.

✦ *Episcopal Public Policy Network.* This service is available from the Episcopal Church's Office of Government Relations. Important information about public policy and advocacy may be accessed through its website.

✦ *Peace and justice ministries of the Episcopal Church.* Information about ministries for national and international justice, support for the environment, and anti-racism training is available through the Episcopal Church's website.

QUESTIONS FOR YOUR CONGREGATION

1. What actions of compassion and outreach are present in your congregation today?

2. How would you describe their effectiveness and impact?

3. Has your congregation done a survey of community needs or met with community agencies and organizations to assess their needs?

4. What might God be calling you to do in service to your neighborhood and wider community?

A CONGREGATION'S STORY

It was a day of real celebration for St. Philip's Church. On this day the congregation was being designated as a "Jubilee Center" by the Episcopal Church. This designation was the result of vision and planning on the part of that congregation as it had established three important ministries of service and outreach: a feeding ministry, a tutoring program, and a housing development corporation (which it shared with other congregations in its neighborhood). Community outreach and service had changed that congregation in its outlook and activity.

It had not always been that way. Sure, there had always been a handful of people interested in issues of peace and justice and community outreach, but the majority of the congregation was more than willing to let this small group bear the responsibility for social conscience in their congregation.

Then things began to change. A family showed up at the church one Sunday morning asking for assistance with food. Instead of simply giving some food from the "pantry closet," two members of the congregation sat down and talked with the mother and her children. They heard her story and the story of their community and decided that they wanted to learn more.

A small group was developed to take the responsibility for learning more about the real situation of their community—and learn they did. They discovered that the three biggest issues were hunger, education, and housing, and they decided to take responsibility for their discovery. The adult education of this congregation became focused on these three areas, and a newly formed outreach committee was charged with finding one response in each area. The responses ended up being a feeding ministry once each week (joining the network of feeding ministries in their community), a tutoring program at the elementary school just down the street, and the structuring of a corporation to develop housing in their neighborhood (again, with other churches in the community). All of it was hard work, and it took time, but these three actions were achieved.

The mission of outreach and compassion has had three major effects. First, important service and compassion is being shown within the community. Second, parish members are being transformed by their activities and commitment to those on the margins. And, finally, these ministries have proven to be an important part of the invitation that this congregation makes to visitors and potential newcomers, truly showing the heart of the congregation.

faithful stewardship

This final mark and characteristic of vital and growing congregations is one that reflects commitment in a very direct way. Stewardship is the thankful offering and response to God for the gifts which God has given to us. Communities of faith are called to be stewards of tradition, facilities, financial resources, and programs. A spirit of stewardship, generosity, and thanksgiving permeates healthy and vital congregations.

Individuals are also called to faithful stewardship. This is a personal matter of faith and trust exhibited by individual believers. Vital and growing congregations engage individual stewardship in two essential ways. First, they communicate a mission that is compelling, visionary, and worthy of support. Second, they assist people in their own journeys of faith as they are formed and grow in spiritual commitment exhibited through stewardship. Congregations need to focus on both of these areas of stewardship formation and practice.

It is a challenging time for stewardship focus in congregational life. Patterns of giving are changing in

American life. Annual pledging is giving way to more project-focused giving. Younger generations do their stewardship in ways that are different from older generations. Many clergy do not feel at ease in their own understanding of money and are uncomfortable asking for a financial commitment from members of the congregation. Effective and vital congregations have opportunities for formation, learning, and prayer related to the meaning of money and stewardship. They present their own mission clearly and demonstrate how the financial offerings of contributors directly fund and support that mission. Stewardship is not a hidden topic in preaching or conversation. Rather, money is seen and interpreted as a vehicle of God's reign.

Some stewardship resources that are available include:

♦ *The Office of Stewardship.* Several resources and conferences are available for local congregations and members from the Episcopal Church's stewardship office.

♦ *The Episcopal Network for Stewardship (TENS).* A national network offering information, training, and encouragement for local congregations.

♦ *The Consortium of Endowed Episcopal Parishes.* This is not for parishes with substantial endowments only. It has some of the best information on stewardship and mission available today.

♦ *"Living With Money."* A program to help people reflect on the meaning of money in their own lives. This work was initiated by the Episcopal Media Center in partnership with other individuals and organizations.

QUESTIONS FOR YOUR CONGREGATION

1. How is the theology and practice of Christian stewardship presented and discussed in your congregation?

2. What do your members say about stewardship and its meaning in their own lives and in the life of the congregation?

3. Is there a leadership statement regarding Christian stewardship that is shared and understood in your congregation?

4. How might stewardship education and interpretation be strengthened?

A CONGREGATION'S STORY

St. John's Episcopal Church is a pastoral size congregation in a regional city. It offers good programs, has lively worship, and is involved in several outreach efforts. Still, there have been financial challenges for the congregation in recent years as some families who had been "pillars" of the congregation moved to retirement settings out of the city or passed away.

St. John's had never really done much about stewardship or its interpretation. The reflection on and expression of stewardship happened once a year with one sermon and the distribution of pledge cards. Parish leaders suspected that things could be done differently but were not sure what to do. The rector noticed that a provincial conference on stewardship that was open to any individuals or congregations was to be held in a hotel only forty-five minutes away. He mentioned this opportunity at a vestry meeting, and two members said they would join him at the conference.

It was a great event. The rector and two vestry members learned two major things at the conference.

First, that stewardship is a spiritual matter about all of the gifts that God gives to human beings, money being a part but not all of stewardship. Second, they learned that there are abundant resources and ideas for the development of stewardship in their own congregation.

These three representatives came back and made a report to the vestry. They said that one of the major things they learned was that stewardship development required commitment and modeling from congregational leadership itself. They convinced their fellow parish leaders to join in a reflection on the meaning of stewardship in a Saturday retreat and to do a statement about their own commitment and practice of stewardship as congregational leaders.

Life at St. John's that year was focused on stewardship in several different ways. An adult education series on stewardship was introduced. The vestry prepared a "narrative budget" that interpreted the annual parish budget in terms of the mission of the congregation. A parish stewardship task group was formed, and a design for a parish visitation program at the time of the Every Member Canvass was prepared. The communication about stewardship was intentional and hopeful. In the fall the rector preached three sermons on stewardship in succession, instead of just one. Parish leaders described their own journey of faith and stewardship during the autumn season. There was even a children's stewardship event that was well received by parents and children alike.

The people of St. John's became more aware of the gifts that God had given them individually and as a community of faith. The Every Member Canvass produced a record result as more people reflected on the call and hope of stewardship. Some of the younger people in the congregation expressed concern about this form of giving but said that they would give it a try, and one young family gave a $25,000 gift for a new parish youth formation program.

The people of St. John's know that they have a way to go, but they are convinced that they are on a journey of stewardship together.

♦ ♦ ♦ ♦ ♦

It is a hopeful time for congregational transformation and change. There are resources for these efforts, and we have growing knowledge about congregational mission and vitality. We have thousands upon thousands of congregations in this country that gather people together for mission, and we have tens of thousands of people who lead, serve, and care for those congregations. Most importantly, we have the gift of the gospel with its stories of hope, life, invitation, and servanthood; stories that call individuals and congregations to mission, and we have the gift of God's Spirit inspiring, guiding, and renewing communities of faith. God transforms and changes us to transform and change the world. It is God's mission, and it is our mission too. It is the journey of transformation and mission for congregations and for individuals. It is our work, our pilgrimage, and our call.

chapter five

Practicing Transformation

God transforms us. It is God's action and power at work in the transformation of individual people and communities of faith. In turn, human beings must appropriate this transformation and live into the structures, patterns, and practices that nurture and represent God's transforming gifts.

Considerable attention has been given to practices of Christian life and community in recent years. This is appropriate for several reasons. A rich heritage and tradition of Christian practices form a basis for living our faith today. Perhaps even more importantly, people in our postmodern context prefer to engage experiences and traditions of faith through practices rather than dogma and doctrine. We live in a period when experience serves as the foundation for believing instead of dogmatic assent. Practice allows Christian faith and transformation to become embodied in individuals and communities of faith. These patterns of active faith join people of faith to a long tradition of Christian living and believing while making the tradition contemporary and accessible.

Robert Wuthnow accurately describes the spirituality of our times as a movement from one of dwelling to one of seeking. He describes the distinction in this way:

> A spirituality of dwelling emphasizes *habitation:* God occupies a definite place in the universe and creates a sacred space in which humans too can dwell; to inhabit sacred space is to know its territory and to feel secure. A spirituality of seeking emphasizes *negotiation:* individuals search for sacred moments that reinforce their conviction that the divine exists, but these moments are fleeting; rather than knowing the territory, people explore new spiritual vistas, and they may have to negotiate among complex and confusing meanings of spirituality.[20]

These two forms of spirituality are not mutually exclusive, but the point is that, in our time, there is movement to a spirituality of seeking, yearning, inquiring, and searching.

In my view, the ancient wisdom that emphasizes the ideal of spiritual practices needs to be rediscovered.... Spiritual practices put responsibility squarely on individuals to spend time on a regular basis worshiping, communing with, listening to, and attempting to understand the ultimate source of sacredness in their lives. —*Robert Wuthnow*

A seeking spirituality depends greatly on spiritual practices as the form of connection and intersection with God. Wuthnow realizes that individual spiritual practices are foundational, but he also points to the practice focused life of congregations:

> Practice-oriented spirituality can best be nurtured by practice-oriented religious organizations—that is, by churches, synagogues, mosques, temples, and other places of worship that define their primary mission as one of strengthening the spiritual disci-

plines of its members. Such organizations will strive to give members both roots and wings—roots to ground them solidly in the traditions of their particular faith, wings to explore their own talents and the mysteries of the sacred. In spiritual practice, religious institutions need to be conceived as facilitators rather than as ends in themselves.[21]

What a vision of the transformative community of faith this is!

practice makes perfect

As my mother said about my approach to the piano when I was a youngster, "Practice makes perfect." Christian practices "perfect" the experience of faith within us. They provide a meaningful structure for our faith, a structure for our own transformation. As you think of your own congregation, you will recognize certain practices, structures, and patterns that build and form Christian faith within you and your companion believers. These practices build community, join us to God, present the Christian story, and assist us in our own transformation.

Some of these are practices of worship and prayer, of biblical and theological reflection. There are also practices of service, evangelism, stewardship, community life, and pastoral ministry found in congregational life. Practices allow people to go deeper into their own faith and experience. They are transformative, giving more than casual or customary expression to Christian believing and living. Practices have the power to transform us as individuals and in Christian community.

Two recent approaches to practices illustrate their importance as structures and means of transformation. The first approach is that of Craig Dykstra and Dorothy Bass in *Practicing Our Faith: A Way of Life for a Searching*

People, a book in which they join with other writers to describe practices which have been part of the Christian experience of transformation since the beginning and remain significant patterns of life today.

In the introduction to *Practicing Our Faith,* Dorothy Bass defines "practices" as "those shared activities that address fundamental human needs and that, woven together, form a way of life."[22] In another related book, Craig Dykstra offers a definition of practices as "those cooperative human activities through which we, as individuals and communities, grow and develop in moral character and substance."[23] The point of both definitions is that practices are patterns of living, praying, and believing which give form and expression to Christian life.

Practicing Our Faith comments on several Christian practices that have existed since the beginning and continue to have powerful expression in Christian communities and the lives of individual believers. These practices are built on even more fundamental ones: prayer, worship, and biblical reflection, and proclamation. The practices identified by Bass and Dykstra include the following.

HONORING THE BODY
The practice of honoring the body focuses on the care and respect we give to our bodies as created physical beings. The Christian tradition has exhibited respect for our physical nature as human beings since the beginning. Today this practice finds expression in wellness, physical renewal, and nutrition considerations. Local congregations engage this practice through teaching, groups and services that tend to physical well being, and responding to human hunger.

A congregation's story
St. Edmund's Church is a congregation in a large city. It is just over a hundred years old and has an average Sunday attendance of 180. Not too long ago, Emma, a long-time member of the congregation, was found on the floor of her home having suffered a serious diabetic incident. Emma had lived alone a long time, and her family was in a distant city. People began to have conversations among themselves and in the pastoral care committee of the congregation.

One of the congregation's pastoral care members had heard that there were a growing number of congregations that were utilizing parish nurses and parish health ministries programs. Another member went to the internet and discovered that they could learn more about a health ministries program for their congregation. They did the legwork, and in a few months they had begun a parish health ministries program. The program includes a part-time nurse who does visits along with lay pastoral care committee members. The program did not end there, though. Health education became a part of the ongoing life of the congregation. As a congregation, they were honoring the body, both the bodies of people and the Body of Christ itself.

HOSPITALITY
Hospitality in a congregation is the practice of openness, invitation, and welcome that reflect the hospitality of God. This practice is rooted in God's hospitality and welcome to us. Congregations offer this practice through evangelism, welcome, and community life that nurtures people in their seeking and searching. Hospitable practice is important in worship and fellowship. A hospitable climate is essential to mission and the invitation of people into the community of faith.

A congregation's story

St. Bartholomew's is a friendly congregation. It has always perceived and represented itself as a warm and caring community, and is the home to some 300 worshipers each Sunday. There is pride in a full range of programs and occasions offered for the congregation and its members.

One Sunday, four people in their twenties were noticed by some long-time members at the end of the service. A conversation began. A church member welcomed them to their first St. Bart's worship. "Actually, this isn't our first visit here," offered one of the visitors in response. "Each of us has been here as individuals, but no one seemed to notice. It's kind of a scary place to visit, so we thought that we would come together."

The last term the people of St. Bartholomew's ever thought applied to their congregation was "scary," but the parish members listened to what these young people had to say. They had not felt welcomed by the music or the worship, and not a single person had talked to them at the coffee hour. Each of these young people wondered if they should return, but they decided to come back together for a last attempt.

The two St. Bart's members talked with others in the congregation and related the story of these young visitors. They realized that very little in their congregation was welcoming to young, single people—and they decided to do something about it. The four young people were contacted and invited to return. People listened to their stories, and the parish decided to learn more so that they might be truly hospitable to the stranger. They began to try different forms of music and worship that reflected the interests of younger generations; they did some advertising in the community's young adult newspaper, and investigated opportunities for specific young adult ministry.

HOUSEHOLD ECONOMICS

The practice of using resources carefully for living faithfully, simply, and well is essential in a culture and time of great consumption and consumerism. American people are in debt at the highest level in our history. Commercial messages bombard us through every possible medium. This practice empowers individuals to make faithful and sensible decisions about their resources, household priorities, and stewardship. A congregation encourages this practice through learning about the meaning of money and other resources (something that is often avoided in congregational life) and the way that decisions about purchases and priorities are made. Several "simple living" resources help individuals and congregations to make decisions and priorities that are rooted in gospel values.

A congregation's story
There had always been an Every Member Canvass every fall at the Church of Our Savior. By and large, it was effective: financial resources were committed to the mission of the congregation. However, there was real discomfort in talking about money and its meaning in our lives.

The Christian Education Committee came across an interesting educational resource that focused on the meaning of money. They decided to use it for an adult education series. The results were encouraging. People had frank conversations about what meaning money had in their lives, in their families, and for their children.

The Church of Our Savior is still living into its encouragement of the practice of household economics among its members. There have been further learning occasions and retreats focused on the meaning and use of resources, financial and otherwise. Parish members are given structures and learning resources to help them make their household decisions. The theme of this year's multigenerational Advent learning will be "Simple living to greet the coming of Christ."

SAYING YES AND SAYING NO

Having moral clarity and making clear decisions is a challenge in this fast-moving and changing world. This practice helps people to make moral decisions in our complex context. There are individual implications to this practice, and there are congregational ones. A congregation is a community of moral formation and learning, as congregations are called to make decisions about their moral presence and leadership in the wider community.

A congregation's story

St. Richard's Church is an urban congregation in a neighborhood that has seen some pretty rough times, but now is a center for renovation and restoration of historic houses. St. Richard's has been faithful throughout. It has assisted in neighborhood service ministries in the lean times and is welcoming new residents in the neighborhood as the community enjoys a renaissance. One of the parish buildings has been empty except for storage for several years.

Now a new use has been proposed by the congregation's members and by other congregations in the city that want to collaborate in a new venture. The vision is to have a feeding and social service ministry housed in the unused space. This is congruent with the tradition of the congregation and certainly needed in the city. However, when the local neighborhood association heard about the proposal, neighbors were enraged. These people had worked hard to reestablish this community as a safe, welcoming place. The neighborhood was more stable but still fragile in many ways from their perspective. Providing a gathering place for low income/no income people could, in their opinion, cause regression to a time of crime and drug-dealing.

St. Richard's had to decide what to do. There were parishioners on both sides of the issue, and it seemed that moral values were in collision with each other. The gospel called this congregation to serve those who were hungry and to love the neighbor. Difficult, soul-searching, moral conversations ensued, and a decision was made. The result after long, hard work is a center that does feed the hungry and a growing, diverse congregation of people, many from the neighborhood itself.

KEEPING SABBATH

Keeping sabbath means making space for God in our hyperactive schedules. Sabbath is as old as God's action in creating the world. It has been a practice for people of faith for millennia. This practice is particularly important in our hectic world. Individuals need to make space for refreshment, renewal, and the experience of God. Congregations are communities of sabbath-keeping. Spiritual space and renewal must overcome the frantic life and pace of many American congregations.

A congregation's story

St. Dunstan's Church was a busy, busy place. It had a multitude of programs, and was open seven days a week. A moderately large congregation, people were ardent in their endeavors. The results were good: it was a church of immense activity. But there were also some problems. People often experienced burnout, and occasionally parish leaders would actually leave the congregation when their particular service or project came to an end. Even the Sunday worship was "fast and furious." There was little silence, and the pace was frantic.

The Worship Committee raised the question first. "Can we slow down?" they asked. They wanted to introduce silence into worship and a pace of prayer that was more deliberate and quiet. It worked. People in the congregation said that Sunday worship was more refreshing and renewing for them. This experience led the priest and vestry to make another decision. During Lent they introduced a Sabbath Day every Wednesday. It was a time for prayer and reflection, for renewal and quiet time alone or together. This had a good effect too. The congregation requested that it continue as a regular part of the life and rhythm of that community of faith.

TESTIMONY
This practice of making witness for the good is a way of "talking the talk and walking the walk." Congruence in belief leads to living and active witness. Testimony is a practice for individuals as they decide what they will affirm, to what values and priorities they will bear witness. It is also a practice for communities of faith as they engage praying and learning which leads to action for justice, peace, and integrity.

A congregation's story
"This is outrageous," said one parish member at St. Matthew's. "How can this happen in such a horrible way in our community?" asked another. These comments were in response to recent events in the community of this near suburban, medium-sized congregation. There had been two immigration raids in their community, and in one of the raids, several families had been detained and handcuffed at a local shopping center. One of the hand-cuffed families was a member family in the growing Latino presence at St. Matthew's.

The congregation decided that it needed to do several things in response to this set of events. First, it prayed for all immigrants, for law enforcement personnel, and for our country. Then, they began to learn in earnest about the issues of legal and illegal immigration. Finally, they made witness in a variety of ways: on their own website, on the sign outside the church, in their Sunday bulletin, and through public witness. Members of the congregation contacted local and national public officials with a clear statement of their experience and commitments.

Not every member of the congregation agreed with this stand. Some people thought it was "unpatriotic" or too "one-sided." The congregation made great efforts to communicate respect to this group as well, so that they would feel included even as the parish made its witness.

DISCERNMENT

Discernment involves listening to and perceiving God's direction and word. How do we know what we are supposed to do? How can we perceive God's wish and will for our lives? What is our call, our purpose, and our personal mission? These are the questions manifest in the Christian practice of discernment. Certainly, they are deeply personal questions for a believer, and the practice of discernment is deeply personal in its intent and import. The local congregation also engages this practice through communal experiences of discernment and mutual inquiry.

A congregation's story
St. Anna's is a congregation averaging about forty-five worshipers per Sunday in its small town setting. The congregation has good leadership, including a part-time clergyperson who is also a teacher in a neighboring town. This community of faith has always offered education and service in its community.

Three matters requiring a decision came to the attention of the congregation's leaders. First, the congregation became aware of the possibility of a new form of local training for ordained and lay leadership in their community of faith. At the same time, a person approached the vestry with the request for discernment of her emerging call to serve as a deacon in the church. Finally, a couple who were beginning to plan their marriage approached them.

The parish leaders recognized that all of these things were opportunities for discernment. One of the vestry members had come across a book by the author Parker Palmer that described a form of discernment called a "clearness committee." The clearness committee process is a disciplined and pastoral form of inquiry which respects the individuals who are bringing a question for discernment.

A group from St. Anna's was trained and began the process with the people who were discerning their own call to diaconal service and to married life. Another group entered the discernment and reflection process offered by the diocese to envision the form of ministry and leadership for the congregation that would be most congruent with its gifts and goals. Discernment took a long time, but it was time well spent. There was a greater sense of clarity and community for these individuals and for the congregation as a whole.

SHAPING COMMUNITIES

The practice of shaping communities involves the formation of faithful spiritual communities. This practice is as old as God's people: leaders have been shaping communities since Moses. This practice is intentional for leaders and local congregations as they shape the mission, identity, climate, and practices of a local community of faith.

A congregation's story

Christ Church was an amiable congregation. It was slightly declining in its membership, and the membership itself was aging. The congregation had adequate resources for its annual budget. About 130 people worshiped there week by week. The congregation had finished an interim period in ordained leadership and had called a new rector.

A few months after arriving, the rector brought up a topic with the congregation's wardens at their regular breakfast meeting. She had a concern that was difficult to articulate. Christ Church was a solid congregation in many ways, and she had been welcomed in a hospitable manner. But... it ended there. There was a general malaise in the congregation. People did not invite others to attend church. Parish occasions were polite but distant.

A decision was made that morning to go in some new directions. The goal would be to create a new climate of community at Christ Church. The rector and wardens decided that the issue would be introduced at the next vestry meeting around the question, "What is God doing here?" The vestry considered the question and came to the realization that their primary purpose was to create and shape community in that congregation. They had been giving all their attention to financial, property, and program matters as a group. Now they were being invited in a new direction, a direction of community and spiritual formation for their congregation.

The first step was an inventory of the life of the congregation. The leaders considered what they believed and what they did as a community. Particular attention was given to worship, learning, service, and community-building events. A transformation began to happen in that congregation. The climate was warmer and more hopeful. People began actively to invite their friends to church. Congregation members asked the question "What is God doing here?" and, together, they discovered that God was doing a great deal.

FORGIVENESS

The practice of forgiving those who have wronged us is utterly essential for the spiritual health and wholeness of individual believers. Jesus called his disciples to forgive others, encouraged them to pray that they might forgive, and exhorted them to be the leaven of forgiveness in the world. Local congregations are laboratories for forgiveness and representatives of forgiveness for members and the wider community. In a time of such alienation and violence, this practice of forgiveness is essential for the peace and transformation of the world.

A congregation's story

It was a very difficult time for St. Francis' Church and its congregation of some 400 worshipers per Sunday. One of the key lay professionals of the church had left after a most disturbing period. He probably would have been terminated had he not gone of his own accord. His behaviors had become increasingly problematic and outside the boundaries of appropriate professional conduct.

However, the most pressing issue was not the conduct of the employee. Rather, it was the life and relationships of that congregation. People were angry, and accusation and recrimination flew openly in several different directions. Announcements had been made and communication had been designed to be as open as possible with the congregation, but still the issue and sentiment festered at St. Francis'.

Shortly after the employee's departure, the rector preached a sermon on forgiveness. The Sunday lectionary reading offered up the parable of a man who was forgiven a great debt and yet was not willing to forgive the tiny debt of another individual. The rector preached on Jesus' call to forgive not once or twice, but repeatedly. It was quite a sermon. People applauded at the end—although three people also stood up and walked out of church.

This sermon was a turning point for the congregation. The rector and associate led a series of adult learning sessions focusing on a book about forgiveness. The clergy and lay pastoral team identified people who were particularly hurt or affected in other ways by the turn of events and contacted all of them to begin the process of forgiveness and reconciliation. In this congregation, people were learning to forgive each other, a learning that affected their daily living as well.

HEALING

The practice of healing encompasses physical, spiritual, and psychological wholeness and well being. Jesus employed the practice of healing regularly—in fact, it was essential to his ministry. This practice also has contemporary expression and power for individuals and communities of faith. Prayer and healing action bring wholeness to people and are at the center of the life of a local community of faith.

A congregation's story

The rector of St. Cuthbert's, a congregation with an average Sunday attendance of about 125 people, introduced a new midweek service: a healing Eucharist. People were invited to come weekly for a special service focused on healing for themselves and for others. The prayers for healing from the *Book of Occasional Services* were used for the event, and it made a difference for people who participated in the service.

Interest in the healing ministry grew. The rector responded affirmatively to requests for healing prayers at the main Sunday service. Education and pastoral care also reflected the growing congregational interest in the ministry of healing.

The greatest test of this emerging focus on healing occurred when the young child of parishioners died suddenly and unexpectedly. The whole set of healing resources were brought to that family by a congregation that had explored in some depth the meaning of God's gifts of wholeness. The pain, loss, and grief were real and intense, but so was the healing response of that congregation. It prayed and showed many actions of healing hope to the family and with each other. Together they entered God's gifts of wholeness and hope.

DYING WELL

We live in a culture that does virtually everything it can to deny death, the transition from this life to the next. The Christian faith is different. We acknowledge death as the way to new life. Individual and community practices around dying and at the time of death give expression to faith in resurrection life.

A congregation's story

The Church of the Transfiguration is a lively congregation with attendance on Sundays averaging 260 people. It had recently made the decision to erect a columbarium in the congregation's garden for the interment of cremated remains. The decision itself was met with thanksgiving and anticipation in the congregation, with the notable exception of an individual who did want "the dead" outside the entrance to the parish hall.

It would have been possible to leave the columbarium as a construction project, but the education committee and clergy were not satisfied with such a conclusion. Instead, they made the decision to use this project as a focus for educational and pastoral ministry. In their conversations, they came to realize that the topic of death was usually avoided in their congregational life as well as in their own lives unless they were immediately confronted with its reality.

The group designed an educational offering focusing on death and dying. Record numbers of congregation members attended. The series focused on the theology and psychology of death, on estates and trusts, on hospice care, and on the Christian tradition and practice of burial. The congregational offering did not end there. Congregants were urged to prepare their own funeral plans and instructions. One service of prayer per month was introduced to focus on remembering the departed of the congregation.

The dedication of the columbarium on All Saints' Day was a grand celebration. People remembered their departed loved ones and were aware of their own mortality as well. Most importantly, there was a vivid sense of the communion of saints in this life and in the life to come.

SINGING OUR LIVES

The practice of engaging in praise and spiritual songs transforms the lives of believers and Christian communities. There are many styles and expressions for this practice. What is common among them is the desire to inspire and transform human beings in their seeking and searching.

A congregation's story

"When does the crying stop?" a recently widowed woman asked the rector of St. Christopher's Church at the end of a Sunday morning worship service. This led to two realizations for that pastor. He recognized that he needed to have pastoral conversation with this woman, whose grief had been stirred by the hymns sung during the service. He also understood as never before just how powerful and evocative music was in the human heart and in the life and development of that community of faith.

The pastor did have several conversations with the woman. He also decided to have a conversation with the musician of that congregation. Together they made a further decision: to enlist the worship committee's help to review the musical life of the congregation. They knew that the congregation was blessed with children and adults who loved to sing and that there was a growing commitment to musical expression in this community of faith. People still talk about the Lenten series focusing on hymns and their meaning. There was a lot of singing, praying, and spiritual reflection and proclamation about some of the hymns and spiritual songs that lifted the soul. The worship committee, musician, and rector also decided that it was time to expand the hymn-singing of the congregation to involve songs from the African-American and Latino traditions. Finally, a Taizé worship service with a totally different form of singing was introduced on a once-a-month basis.

St. Christopher's loves to sing. Its members and visitors know the transforming power of music. They want to sing, and they want to grow in their singing to praise God and to strengthen their own bonds of community.

♦   ♦   ♦   ♦   ♦

Together the essays included in Bass and Dykstra's book *Practicing Our Faith* provide a portrait of full and rich life and faith lived out in daily patterns, forms, and actions. These are the ways that people live into their faith as well. The practices themselves connect with the heart, with yearning, seeking, and searching in the core of people today. These practices are also integral to a congregation, as the congregation embodies and exhibits them in its communal journey in faith. They are direct ways and patterns for people to experience the gospel and transformation within local communities of faith, embodying a full engagement of Christian life in worship, Bible reading and reflection, and prayer. The point is that people who participate in local communities of faith experience their own transformation as they engage in these practices and patterns of faith and life.

practices for younger generations

A second approach to spiritual practices in the congregation can be seen in the practices employed by young people and their leaders in a Lilly Endowment funded project on spiritual practices for younger generations. The Youth Ministry and Spirituality Project builds on the identification of practices as a foundational mode of Christian faith and action by asking how practices form and inform the spiritual life of young people. The goal of the project is to shape a way of life that will sustain young people in the present and the future.[24]

> Christian practices are the *means* through which Christians seek to respond to God's invitations of love. They are the habits, disciplines, and patterns of life through which Christians seek communion with Christ and solidarity with others.
> —K. Creasy Dean, C. Clark, and D. Rahn

The practices used in the Youth Ministry and Spirituality Project include the following:

• *Three commitments:* daily prayer, spiritual direction, and an *examen* on ministry

A committed and intentional Christian life and walk are the foundation for these practices. Each one of them is intended to draw people closer to God and to the love of God. Daily prayer can be done in a variety of styles and expressions. The important thing is that there is a daily practice of praying that causes people to stop, to recollect the presence of God, and to be joined to the love of God. Spiritual direction is establishing an ongoing relationship with a spiritual director. This practice acknowledges the importance of spiritual friendship and perspective offered by another for spiritual growth and renewal. The *examen* is an intentional look at what is happening in personal progress toward spiritual goals and the expression of personal mission and ministry.

+ *Lectio divina:* the reflective engagement of Holy Scripture, a practice rooted deep in the Christian tradition.

This is a different kind of scriptural "reading" and encounter. The goal of *lectio divina* is to spend focused time on a story or portion of scripture in a way that allows the reader to actually enter the narrative and meaning of the story.

+ *Centering prayer:* a quiet, intentional form of prayer.

This mode of prayer is not fast-moving public prayer. Rather, it is quiet, focused prayer that allow a person to prayerfully "breathe" with the breath of God.

+ *Awareness examen:* emerging from the Ignatian spiritual tradition, a process of reviewing and examining daily thought, feeling, and action in terms of how God seemed to be present and how we responded to that presence.

+ *Awareness examen over youth ministry:* the monthly practice of an awareness *examen* focusing on the ministry and community itself, done with others in the community. While this practice is focused on youth ministry, the awareness *examen* may be done over any particular ministry that is the primary call and mission of a person of faith.

This spiritual practices approach to ministry with young people envisions a new and transforming style and type of youth ministry. The building of community, social relationships, and service experiences remain important, but the vision of this form of youth ministry asserts something different. Young people and those who minister to them are invited to go more deeply into faith through spiritual practices and to connect with the heart's seeking and searching through them.

The practices identified in the Youth Ministry and Spirituality Project are of traditional and current significance. They are patterns of spiritual life that form people and assist in their transformation. They are ancient patterns that can be employed in the present moment as a bridge to transformation for individuals and for communities.

◆   ◆   ◆   ◆   ◆

The spiritual and communal practices identified by both Craig Dykstra and Dorothy Bass and the people who shaped the Youth Ministry and Spirituality Project intersect with the practices of congregational life and transformation described in previous chapters. For example, spiritual practices of discernment shape the congregational practices of leadership, mission articulation, vision, and planning. The spiritual practice of hospitality shapes the congregational practices of proclamation, evangelism, and recruitment. The spiritual practices of *lectio divina,* meditation, and contemplation/*examen* shape the congregational practices of prayer, learning, and formation. There are other examples of the close relationship between spiritual practices and congregational life practices. All of them contribute to the life and transformation of people and communities of faith.

the practice of leadership

One of the most important practices actually develops these other practices and is responsible for the climate of transformation within a community of faith. That is the practice of leadership. Transformed and transforming communities of faith require faithful and effective leadership. The leadership of a congregation is essential to its vitality and mission. Leadership makes decisions, sets a healthy and hopeful tone for community life, develops resources, articulates the mission, envisions and plans for the future, and builds relationships within the congregation and between that community of faith and other entities.

Leadership is a big job and an important responsibility. It molds and shapes a community of faith. There are clergy leaders, lay professional leaders, and lay leaders in varieties of leadership roles: vestries, boards, commissions, committees, ministry, teams, and small groups, just to name a few. The congregation's leadership frames the environment and climate of a community of faith. Particularly in times of stress, the leadership plays the important role of keeping balance and forward movement rather than being sucked into anxiety, anger, and instability.

As in congregational life more generally, certain practices of leadership employed on an ongoing basis help congregational leaders in times of particular challenge and stress. These practices include the following:

+ Clarity of purpose and mission.

Leaders need to spend the time necessary to clarify the basic mission and purpose of the local community of faith. It is important for the ongoing life and work of a congregation and is especially important in times of challenge and dis-equilibrium. Clearly, clarity of mission and purpose is at the heart of congregational vitality and growth. The leadership of the congregation has primary responsibility for this clarity. They need to engage an intentional process of determining their mission and its priorities. The responsibility continues with the communication of the mission and measuring of programs and activities in relationship to the mission and its purpose.

• Intentional leadership of transformation and change.

Congregational leadership is continuously involved in change and in the leadership of change. Leaders need to understand this responsibility and have systems and plans in place for change and transformation. Congregational leaders cannot settle for the status quo. They are responsible for meeting and engaging change in an environment of growing cultural and ecclesial transition. Leadership is at the frontline in meeting these often challenging and unexpected changes. An equal part of the work of leadership is planning change for a congregation. A strategy for change frames the possibility of transformation which is a gift from God.

• Creating and building relationships.

Leadership is relational at its very core today and involves invitation, mutuality, and partnership. Congregational leadership is deeply involved in the creation and nurture of relationships that build community and sustain people in their living. One of the marks of vital and strong congregations is the quality of caring. Leaders model and encourage caring relationships that fortify people's lives. Congregational leaders have the privilege of building many relationships for mission. The majority of them are within the congregation itself. People are joined together in community to engage and further God's mission in that place. Leaders encourage the development of a fabric of relationship throughout the congregation. They also exercise their own leadership in terms of the authority that comes from relationship rather than structure, law, or custom.

+ A learning stance.

Learning is important in times of massive change. Leadership needs to model a stance of learning which leads to transformation. Part of this is the leadership learning undertaken by those who exercise this function in the community of faith. Congregational leaders are responsible for their own education in leadership and for modeling learning interest and dispositions within the local congregation. They also need to shape the values and climate of the congregation around learning for all ages. Leaders learn, and they contribute to the learning environment of the congregation. Learning itself contributes to the depth of congregational life and potential for growth and vitality. The congregation's leaders are responsible for a design for learning for all ages in the congregation. They are also responsible for monitoring the expression and effectiveness of learning and for the design of their own learning progress and program as a leadership team.

+ Clear, confident, consistent, collaborative.

In their "Toward a Higher Quality of Christian Ministry" project, project directors John Dreibelbis and David Gortner identified these characteristics of leaders as essential for clergy. They were researching clergy leadership, but the characteristics apply to all leadership in communities of faith. Patterns of clarity in communication and consistency in action build trust. Collaboration allows for movement in mission together. Probably the most important of these characteristics is confidence. Leaders require confidence in God, in the gospel, in their own community, and in their own capacities. Congregational leaders must make decisions. In many congregations this is a challenge. People are timid about leadership and often fear making decisions that might prompt some negative reaction. Often leaders do not show the same quality of decision-making in church settings as they do in other parts of life. Congregational leaders need to claim the authority of the gospel and of their own mission so that they can make decisions that move the congregation more fully into its mission and call.

+ Vision and hope.

Leaders need to create a vision for the future and embody hope. Recent leadership studies have demonstrated that an attitude of hope is essential to the practices of a leadership that works from the bases of assets and strengths rather than problems and inadequacies. There is a demonstrable difference in effectiveness between those congregations that portray a hopeful vision and those that are pessimistic. Leaders model and set the tone for the great local community of faith. Congregational leaders have a particular responsibility for envisioning the future mission of their community of faith. There are many sources for that vision: imagination, scripture, ideas offered by congregational members themselves. Leaders are the people in a congregation who bring these sources together and envision future mission. They have further responsibility as well, planning and developing strategy for mission and evaluating its effectiveness.

These practices help to sustain leadership within a local community of faith. They also help to resist particular challenges in the life of local communities: parish conflict, mission paralysis, leadership (clergy and lay) burnout, and distraction. Leaders practice their leadership for their own fulfillment and for the ongoing mission of a congregation.

This chapter has included a broad consideration of practices that enhance and contribute to the transformation of people and communities of faith. At their foundation are three basic assertions about spirituality in the twenty-first century.

1. God is at work in the world and in people's lives through God's mission of restoration, reconciliation, and renewal.

2. Spirituality of the twenty-first century is characterized by seeking, searching, and inquiry.

3. The church must nurture and respect differing styles of spiritual inquiry and experience.

The first assumption affirms that God is at work; God's purpose and mission are active. That is a foundational theological tenet, and it is equally substantial as a tenet of spirituality. God's activity is not hemmed in or bounded by anything in the world or the church. This has always been the case, but it is particularly significant for us to remember as we enter the twenty-first century. In a time of such immense change and transition, it behooves us to look even more carefully for God's presence and action. Instead of assuming that God is absent due to this rapid change, we would do better to focus on God in the change, to the ways that God is transforming the world, the church, and human beings. To approach postmodern, twenty-first-century spirituality is to approach the mystery of God's actions of mission and transformation in the lives and experiences of human beings.

The framework of spiritual experience itself has also moved from one of certainties and dicta to one of seeking, searching, and inquiry. It is truly an amazing thing in

American culture that when people are surveyed they respond by talking about belief in God, spiritual experience, and seeking and yearning for the mystery of God. However, there is a serious disconnect between this profound spiritual interest and inquiry, and religious institutions and structures. This has been described in great detail in the reflection on the spirituality of young adults in Robert Fuller's important book *Spiritual, But Not Religious*. The author focuses on the spiritual experience of young people and the way that religious institutions have missed the connection with that spirituality of seeking and searching. However, the case may be made much more broadly in our context and society. There is significant spiritual seeking and experience that have been overlooked by religious institutions which seem too inflexible, hidebound, and committed to infighting.

Fuller describes people who are "spiritual, but not religious" as "rejecting traditional organized religions as the sole—or even most valuable—means of furthering spiritual growth." He notes that many people have had negative experiences with churches or church leaders, perhaps even in the form of emotional or sexual abuse. These individuals have therefore forsaken formal religious institutions and organizations, and "have instead embraced an individualized spirituality that includes picking and choosing from a wide range of alternative religious philosophies. They typically view spirituality as a journey intimately linked with the pursuit of personal growth or development."[25]

We see these patterns at work in our own society. People identify spiritual practices and journey as a part of their experience, but they are reluctant to join a traditional congregation. They are seeking, and their seeking requires response from the church. The response itself is one that centers on the search and on the spiritual experience of God. Those congregations that are learning to engage these realities are intersecting more effectively and fully with the postmodern world and experience itself.

One of the most helpful reflections on the mission of the church in postmodern culture is offered by Eddie Gibbs and Ryan Bolger in their book *Emerging Churches*. They recognize the seeking spirituality of our culture and time and call for a church that is alive in and focused on mission. They envision and describe mission-focused communities of faith that recognize the seeking and searching of people and focus on hospitality and inclusion (rather than much of exclusion present in the modern version of church life). Practices of inclusion (particularly Eucharistic worship, hospitality, creation of a "safe place," welcoming those who are different, and transparent humility) invite and incorporate seekers. Gibbs and Bolger call for a church with an "embodied apologetic and a clear reliance on the Holy Spirit to guide, lead, and carry the agenda."[26] Individuals and communities of faith are transformed. Lives are changed. Grace is "spoken through lives."

Spirituality is a major emphasis in emerging churches, more important than numbers gathered or even the celebrative nature of the worship. The real concerns are the extent to which lives are changed and gaining depth through the richness of encounters with God.
— *Eddie Gibbs and Ryan Bolger*

A practice-oriented, seeking spirituality is at the root and foundation of this transformation. Ancient spiritualities are rediscovered, *and* they are joined to contemporary holistic and mystical spirituality. Practices are employed to ground people deeply in the faith and create flexibility for the dance of the spirit.

Gibbs and Bolger note that "the real concerns are the extent to which lives are changing and gaining depth through the richness of encounters with God." I cannot think of a clearer description of the spirituality of transformation or of the transforming purpose, call, and mission of God's church. The issue is the extent of transformation and depth through transformation. Churches that offer opportunities, experiences, and encounters of transformation are living out their mission and demonstrate considerable attributes of strength and vitality. That's why people come to church. That's why people become invested in a community of faith.

> Members of emerging churches recognize that there is no instant formula. Rather, spiritual disciplines have to be learned through costly exploration. They draw upon a variety of traditions and combine them in a creative mix. — *Eddie Gibbs and Ryan Bolger*

Understanding the seeking, searching, and inquiry dimensions of postmodern spirituality does not mean that every congregation must radically change its patterns of worship, proclamation, and community life. It does mean that every congregation must reflect on how it welcomes such seeking and searching, that every congregation must give attention to serving and inviting the vast number of people who seek God but who are outside the community of the local church.

The mode of this invitation and hospitality is found in the third of the spirituality assertions for the twenty-first century: we must respect and nurture varieties of styles of spirituality. This begins with awareness that there is indeed a broad variety of spiritual styles. Richard Foster raises this awareness by describing the wide range of spiritual styles and traditions in his study *Streams of Living Water*. Most importantly, he perceives a great flow of spiritual power today.

Today a mighty river of the Spirit is bursting forth from the hearts of women and men, boys and girls. It is a deep river of divine intimacy, a powerful river of holy living, a dancing river of jubilation in the

Spirit, and a broad river of unconditional love for all peoples. . . . Today our sovereign God is drawing many streams together that heretofore have been separated from one another.[27]

This image of a river relates to the basic baptismal and missional theology and practices described in this book. It is a mighty river, like that described in the Psalms, "a river flowing from the throne of God." This river has power and strength. It also has a variety of currents, streams, and tributaries. This is the river of spiritual experience and practice in the twenty-first century. There are many currents and styles, streams and experiences, tributaries and emphases. No one way is the only way for people today.

The congregation that reflects this variety and allows for different experiences grows in depth and often in the interest and participation of people. Congregations that limit and insist on one style or set of experiences do not enjoy the same depth. Part of the work of congregational leadership is to introduce and encourage participation in a variety of styles. Part of the commitment of the individual's life of faith is to approach different practices and styles for his or her own spiritual enrichment.

Practices lead to transformation for communities of faith and for individuals. The human heart itself is transformed through practices that introduce and enhance the experience of God. People are changed. Their view of the world, their experience of daily living, their relationships and vision for the future—all are changed and transformed through their experience and intersection with God through these various practices. It is, in fact, the grounding of life in God and in God's Spirit. The result is a journey that reflects God's gifts of hospitality, forgiveness, refreshment, and service.

It is a time of spiritual inquiry and experience in American life. For the life and leadership of the church that means several things. First, it means that focus on practices of Christian community and spiritual experience is essential for this time. Second, it means that special attention needs to be given to the practices of leadership. Much depends on the development of leadership in the life of the local community of faith, and its mission and purpose will be enhanced through attention to leadership practice and enhancement. Finally, it means that intentional effort must be given to being a community of invitation and hospitality that recognizes and respects the spiritual searching and seeking that is going on inside and outside our congregations.

The practices identified in the chapter are at the foundation for congregations in mission. They are modes of transformation for individuals and for congregations themselves. God is experienced in them, and God transforms human beings through them. These practices strengthen mission. They build capacities for mission. They are transformative, transforming people and communities for mission, and, through them, fortifying the mission of transforming the world.

effecting change, getting started

Congregations are the frontline of mission for the church in the American culture in our present day. Congregational mission is transformational by its very nature. People are changed, community is transformed, and the human heart itself is restored and renewed through congregational mission. It is the purpose of congregations. Congregations can change to be transformed communities of mission, vitality, and strength.

However, not all congregations are in the place where they want to change. Some simply do not see the need for it; others fear the uncertainty. Transformation is powerful but messy. Yet if we are to survive and grow we must change—as congregations, as leaders, as the church itself. John Kotter has written one of the most important books about the dynamics of change and organizational leadership for and in the midst of change. In *Leading Change* he describes the fear of change in organizations large and small in this way:

> People who have been through difficult, painful, and not very successful change efforts often end up drawing both pessimistic and angry conclusions. They become suspicious of the motives of those pushing for transformation; they worry that major change is not possible without carnage. . . . I draw a different conclusion. Available evidence shows that most public and private organizations can be significantly improved . . . but that we often make terrible mistakes when we try because history has simply not prepared us for transformational challenges.[28]

So how do congregations prepare for transformational challenges and changes, indeed, for transformation itself? Kotter suggests that urgency is the place to begin. Very little will change without a sense of urgency in any organization, including the church. The congregation that is complacent will usually not be transformed or transforming for people. Complacency may be a result of fear, lethargy, denial, or avoidance. It is always debilitating for a congregation.

There are a host of reasons for a sense of urgency in congregational life. Some of those reasons may be numerical. Membership, attendance, and giving may be slipping at a slow or rapid rate. It is harder to recruit and retain members, leaders, and volunteers in congregational mission. There is a sense of dis-ease in the congregational life itself. The gospel may have lost it punch.

All of these are reasons for claiming and articulating a sense of urgency in congregational life, but they do not include the most urgent reason of all: the gospel. The gospel is urgent and demands urgent response. It is Good News to be proclaimed, shared, and lived. This is urgent business. Declining numbers and insufficient funds are not sufficient reasons for change and urgency in congregational life. They can be used as indicative factors, and if a congregation analyzes them, they help that congregation to see the reality of its present circumstances. No, the real urgency is the gospel and its proclamation of God's love, and with that, the call for local communities of faith to announce that love and invite people to that love. The real urgency is the mission of the church itself calling believers to service, compassion, and transformation.

The congregation (and particularly its leaders) needs to decide that it is going to begin or intensify work in areas of vitality in an urgent way. It realizes that response to the change around it is an urgent matter. It also must realize that the primary congregational vocation of transformation and change has to take a planned and concrete form in its practices and actions.

John Kotter then describes seven other dimensions and stages in the progress of intentional leadership for and in the midst of change. They include:

1. *Creating a guiding coalition:* putting together a group with enough power to lead the change and equipping them to work as a team.

2. *Developing a vision and a strategy:* envisioning the future and developing a strategy for the goals and steps that will lead into that future.

3. *Communicating the change vision:* finding many ways of communicating the new vision and using the coalition for that purpose.

4. *Empowering broad-based action:* working through obstacles and resistance and empowering movement for change and transformation.

5. *Generating short-term wins:* planning for, acknowledging, and affirming improvements and visible actions that embody the hoped-for future.

6. *Consolidating gains and producing more change:* reinforcing actions and removing those elements that are not consistent and congruent with a new culture.

7. *Anchoring new approaches in the culture:* consistently interpreting the new character of the culture, articulating the connections between new behaviors and organizational success, and developing various means to ensure leadership development and succession.

Again, the congregations described in the third and fourth chapters embodied the majority of these elements in their transformation and change processes. Particularly, these congregations did the following:

* They created communities of leadership (what Kotter calls a "guiding coalition").

In the vast majority of them, vestry transformation began prior to congregational transformation. While the vestry might not ultimately be the group responsible for change in a particular area, this church board (whatever it may be called) is responsible for the mission articulation, culture, vision, and mission strategy of the congregation. The kind of transformation and change sought in congregational vitality and renewal must begin with the board of the congregation, the vestry itself. Some means of transforming learning and training is required for these leaders.

The board is not the only community of leadership that would take responsibility for congregational transformation in a local community of faith. "Guiding coalitions" can include other groups, committees, and task forces. These groups may use a particular focus area such as evangelism or education to become a catalyst for transforming change in a congregation. Similarly, a long-range or strategic planning committee may function in this way. The most important thing is that such a coalition/group assumes the responsibility for vision, plan, and progress of change in a congregation.

+ They had clarity of vision and developed a plan for that vision.

Positive change and transformation does not just happen. It requires an inviting and compelling vision presented by leaders in a congregation. The vision, in turn, leads to a plan. It might be a plan for one area of congregational vitality and renewal, or might be a plan for the future of the congregation as a whole. This time of change in the culture and society around us will not allow most congregations to pursue business as usual. Effective congregations move ahead in vision and planning for their mission.

+ Communication was at the very center of congregational transformation.

The effective congregations described in these chapters decided on what they wanted to communicate and did it with intention and regularity. Some congregations used existing modes of communication within the church. Others developed whole new strategies and vehicles for communication.

+ These congregations kept track of their progress.

The group which served as the primary "guiding coalition" did regular review of progress, noted successes, dealt with challenges, and revised the plan as necessary.

Transformation depends on perseverance as much as inspiration (perhaps even more).

◆ The culture was transformed.

Congregations that embody the strengths and vitality described in the third and fourth chapters were not content simply to do the same old things somewhat better. That does not change a congregation and its mission. Especially in a time of rapid, whitewater change, a congregation must seek and enact true change so that the culture is transformed.

For most of the congregations described here, the change in culture occurred in quite deep ways. Some changed the culture of leadership within the congregation through the work of mission definition and leadership training. They moved from church boards as "technical" managers to a culture of leadership focusing on and planning for the mission of the congregation. Other congregations changed the culture of warm welcome into a culture of intentional invitation and radical hospitality. They began and anchored a culture of evangelism and recruitment in the life of the church. This went beyond a norm of being a "friendly" church to practices of invitation, recruitment, faith story telling, and incorporation.

One congregation discovered that it could change the culture of ministries and compassion from that of occasional charity to a spirit of advocacy involving a much greater proportion of congregation members. Some congregations worked to change the culture of giving and stewardship from one of "annual fund-raising" to a spirituality of stewardship and commitment that permeated the congregation and its life throughout the year and formed people in their own attitudes about the meaning of money.

◆ These congregations sought to anchor the change that had been introduced in the ongoing life of the congregation.

This was not occasional programmatic change. It was change for the long-term penetrating to the depth of the mission and life of the congregation itself. Congregational change takes intention and effort. It requires a commitment for the long-haul. Such change can substantially strengthen and enhance congregational mission and vitality. It is a manifestation of congregational transformation.

The present environment requires this kind of transformation. Certainly tradition is important during this time of change, and traditional practices of faith and mission can be utilized in the present time of change. However, the key to the utilization of traditions and practices is the intentional assessment of how they work in the present context. Too many congregations uncritically do things as they always have while believing that this application and honoring of tradition completes their mission responsibility. And those congregations wonder: Why are we not moving on in our mission? Why is attendance and commitment declining? Why are new people not being attracted to our congregation and its life?

What is called for is this: a vision of and resources for congregational transformation. What is needed is this: a commitment to the strengthening and revitalization of existing congregations and the planting of new energetic ones. Most of the responsibility for this transformation resides with the local congregation itself, but the responsibility does not end there. It permeates the work and purpose of the larger church as it enters the twenty-first century. This requires specific tasks and areas of focus for manifestations of the larger church.

For the middle-level judicatory ("dioceses" in the Episcopal Church) it means that one of the primary areas of focus is on the local congregation. Every diocese should have a congregational development function (preferably with an officer and a similar function "with committee" for evangelism). It is the diocesan responsibility to build networks for congregational vitality and to provide useful resources, vision, and support for the development of its congregations of every size and context.

Similarly, it is the responsibility of the national judicatory (the denomination) to organize itself to serve local congregations with support, resources, and training. Some of that is done through dioceses. Much of it is done with the local congregation through mechanisms of training and resource development. This service also involves an intentional listening to the needs, experience, and successes of local congregations. At present, the Episcopal Church is transforming its organizational life to serve congregations and their leaders in ever more direct and useful ways.

One other set of institutions that have a broader responsibility for resources to congregations, their leaders, and their transformation are the seminaries of the church. Their purpose is to form leaders for mission, leaders who are grounded in faith and tradition, *and* who are equally prepared in congregational development and leadership. As congregations must change, so these institutions must become more focused on this primary purpose and engage new ways of forming and equipping leaders for congregational transformation. It is a sea change for seminaries of the Episcopal Church. There will be fewer of them, and they will be changed in their focus.

It is essential for these manifestations of the church to focus on congregational strength and vitality and the development of leadership for this strength and vitality. There are other important issues in the life of the church to be sure, but the health, strength, and vitality of local communities of faith is uniquely significant. Strong congregations are the locus for progress in mission more broadly. They are the models and manifestations of the gospel imperatives of hospitality, service, and proclamation.

What about your congregation? Where is it in its transformation and growth in strength and vitality? Where is it in its mission? Ultimately the question of congregational mission, strength, and vitality comes to each local community of faith. It is up to the leaders and members of local congregations to assess and envision the mission and effectiveness of that congregation. Theory and theology have a use to be sure, but the real test of reflection and learning about congregational mission and transformation is in your congregation itself. Will you and your fellow leaders engage in a prayerful, planned, and intentional process of change and transformation for your congregation and, through your congregation, for its members and for the world outside your church doors? What about your own life? Where are you in your journey of faith, service, and leadership? Where are you in your personal mission and transformation as a person of faith?

Ultimately, these are the significant questions for this time of hope for congregations and for the members of congregations themselves. It is a time for change and a call to transformation for congregations and for individual Christian people. God is transforming us. God is changing us.

> O God of unchangeable power and eternal light: Look favorably on your whole Church, that wonderful and sacred mystery; by the effectual working of your providence, carry out in tranquillity the plan of salvation; let the whole world see and know that things which were cast down are being raised up, and things which had grown old are being made new, and that all things are being brought to their perfection by him through whom all things were made, your Son Jesus Christ our Lord. Amen. (BCP 280)

A Guide for
Discussion

You may of course read the books in this series on your
own, but because they focus on the transformation of
the Episcopal Church in the twenty-first century the
books are especially useful as a basis for discussion and
reflection within a congregation or community. The questions below are intended to generate fruitful discussion
about the congregations with which members of the
group are familiar.

Each group will identify its own needs and will be
shaped by the interests of the participants and their
comfort in sharing personal life stories. Discussion leaders
will wish to focus on particular areas that address the
concerns and goals of the group, using the questions and
themes provided here simply as suggestions for a place to
start the conversation.

Shall We Gather at the River?

In this chapter James Lemler explores the theology of baptism and how it has shaped the mission of the church. He notes that "baptismal theology is a theology of transformation and mission, emphasizing both the change that occurs in the life of individual believers and the meaning of mission for the church" (p. 9).

* In what ways has baptism—your own or others—been part of your formation and sense of ministry?

* How is a theology of baptism expressed and lived in your congregation?

* Name several ways you seek to live out the Baptismal Covenant in your congregation and community.

✦　✦　✦　✦　✦

In exploring a renewed theology of mission Lemler quotes the hopeful vision of Darrell Guder (pp. 16–17). He goes on to describe several efforts made at the diocesan and national levels that reflect an emerging theology of mission in the church today.

* What do you make of Guder's optimism? Have you seen reasons to share his hope for the future of the local and national church?

* What do you think of the various national efforts Lemler describes, such as "A Clear Vision," the 2020 Vision, and the mission priorities set forth by General Convention? Which aspects of these approaches to mission are most important to you? What is missing?

* If you were developing a list of mission priorities for your congregation, what would you include?

Whitewater Conditions

Lemler opens this chapter with a discussion of the gospel as transformation. He then explores Parker Palmer's ten points that can help congregations move "away from the shadows that paralyze them to new light, new trust, and new love" (p. 39).

♦ Reread the five "shadows" and reflect on the ways they may have hindered transformation and growth in your congregation.

♦ Reread the five "lights" and reflect on some of the ways they may have encouraged transformation and growth in your congregation.

♦ ♦ ♦ ♦ ♦

Lemler then turns to the "whitewater conditions" churches find themselves in today, looking at fifteen dimensions of the changing environment (pp. 43–50).

♦ Review these conditions for change and select several that you believe are the most pressing for your congregation. Why are they significant at this time?

♦ How do the particular "whitewater conditions" you have identified affect the mission of your congregation?

♦ ♦ ♦ ♦ ♦

Finally, Lemler examines the results of two important surveys on congregational life (pp. 51–61).

♦ What do you make of these results? Do they reflect your congregation's experience?

♦ Which results were surprising to you? Which are the most challenging for your congregation?

The Vital Congregation

In this chapter Lemler considers five characteristics of a healthy congregation: clarifying mission; spiritual transformation; context and congregational dynamics; learning; and evangelism and welcome.

+ Divide into five small groups or pairs, and assign one characteristic to each group. (If necessary, groups can take on more than one characteristic.) The person in each small group who agrees to be the scribe needs to be given writing materials.

+ Spend at least 20 minutes in small groups, discussing how each characteristic is a strength or a challenge in your congregation. Focus especially on the "questions for your congregation" provided within each section, with the scribe making summary notes of the responses.

+ Reconvene the entire study group, and ask each small group or pair to share its findings. If possible, gather these findings on newsprint or other media for all to see.

+ After each group has shared its findings, spend time reflecting on the picture of your congregation that has emerged.

NOTE:

+ If you are reading this book on your own, simply choose the characteristics that you believe are the most challenging for your congregation and reflect on the questions within those sections.

Communities of Transformation

In this chapter Lemler continues his consideration of the characteristics of a healthy congregation, this time focusing on worship and preaching; leadership development; dealing with conflict; a hopeful climate and flexibility toward change; a caring community; compassionate service; and stewardship.

◆ Divide into seven small groups or pairs, and assign one characteristic to each group. (If necessary, groups can take on more than one characteristic.) The person in each small group who agrees to be the scribe needs to be given writing materials.

◆ Spend at least 20 minutes in small groups, discussing how each characteristic is a strength or a challenge in your congregation. Focus especially on the "questions for your congregation" provided within each section, with the scribe making summary notes of the responses.

◆ Reconvene the entire study group, and ask each small group or pair to share its findings. If possible, gather these findings on newsprint or other media for all to see.

◆ After each group has shared its findings, spend time reflecting on the picture of your congregation that has emerged.

NOTE:

◆ If you are reading this book on your own, simply choose the characteristics that you believe are the most challenging for your congregation and reflect on the questions within those sections.

chapter five

Practicing Transformation

Here Lemler focuses on specific practices that allow the experience of transformation "to become embodied in individuals and communities of faith" (p. 127).

♦ Using the practices given here as a model, develop a list of practices that are significant aspects of your congregational life. Divide into small groups or pairs, with each choosing one practice to discuss.

♦ In the small groups, using the stories on pages 131–144 as models, write the "story" of how your congregation came to see the practice you chose as important to its life and mission, and how it is expressed and encouraged today.

♦ Reconvene in the entire group and share your stories. What themes do you hear emerging?

♦   ♦   ♦   ♦   ♦

Lemler concludes with a consideration of the leadership and concrete actions needed to implement change.

♦ Does your congregation and particularly its leaders see change as an urgent matter? Why or why not?

♦ Review John Kotter's "stages in the progress of intentional leadership for and in the midst of change" identified on pages 159–160. Which ones are the most challenging for your congregation?

♦ How would you respond to Lemler's final question: "Will you and your fellow leaders engage in a prayerful, planned, and intentional process of change and transformation for your congregation?" (p. 165). What is hindering you from getting started?

Resources

---

websites and organizations

There are some excellent sites and resources on congregational development and transformation available from the World Wide Web. They are, however, a "moving target," with information changing regularly. Use a reliable search engine like Google and a good word search.

THE ALBAN INSTITUTE

www.alban.org

An independent center of learning and leadership development with a focus on congregations. Located in greater Washington, D.C., Alban is a not-for-profit, membership organization that develops and shares knowledge through consulting, publishing, research, and education programs.

THE CENTER FOR CONGREGATIONS

www.centerforcongregations.org

This Indianapolis-based center has roots in the Alban Institute and in the Lilly Endowment, Inc. Its focus is useful resources for congregations, their life, and their development. Although its consultation services are limited to the state of Indiana, its knowledge- and resource-base is full and extensive.

CONGREGATIONAL LIFE AND EVANGELISM CENTER: THE EPISCOPAL CHURCH

www.episcopalchurch.org

The work of congregational development, evangelism resources, and congregational research is available at this website. It is framed in very useful ways for local congregations of all sizes and settings.

THE U.S. CONGREGATIONAL LIFE SURVEY

www.uscongregations.org

You can access the learning from the U.S. Congregational Life Survey and tools for congregational revitalization and development at this website.

THE WABASH CENTER

www.resourcingchristianity.org

The Wabash Center has its roots in the Lilly Endowment and assists in leadership and learning development. It sponsors this comprehensive site about resources for Christian leadership and communities of faith.

THE EVANGELICAL LUTHERAN CHURCH IN AMERICA

www.elca.org

The ELCA makes its resources in organizational development and planning available on its website.

books

Bass, Diana Butler. *Christianity for the Rest of Us: How the Neighborhood Church is Transforming the Faith.* San Francisco: HarperOne, 2006.

————. *The Practicing Congregation: Imagining a New Old Church.* Herndon, Va.: Alban Institute, 2004.

Bass, Diana Butler, and Joseph Stewart-Sicking, eds. *From Nomads to Pilgrims: Stories from Practicing Congregations.* Herndon, Va.: Alban Institute, 2005.

Bass, Dorothy, ed. *Practicing Our Faith: A Way of Life for a Searching People.* San Francisco: Jossey-Bass, 1997.

Bass, Richard. *www.congregationalresources.org: A Guide to Resources for Building Congregational Vitality.* Herndon, Va.: The Alban Institute, 2005.

Bliese, Richard H., and Craig Van Gelder, ed. *The Evangelizing Church: A Lutheran Contribution.* Minneapolis: Augsburg-Fortress, 2005.

Callahan, Kennon. *Effective Church Leadership: Building on the Twelve Keys.* San Francisco: Harper & Row, 1990. *(This is but one book by this prolific writer in congregational vitality and development.)*

Gibbs, Eddie, and Ryan K. Bolger. *Emerging Churches: Creating Christian Community in Postmodern Cultures.* Grand Rapids: Baker Publishing, 2005.

Hawkins, Thomas R. *The Learning Congregation.* Louisville: Westminster John Knox, 1997.

Herrington, Jim, Mike Bonem, and James Furr. *Leading Congregational Change: A Practical Guide for the Transformational Journey.* San Francisco: Jossey-Bass, 2000.

Hopewell, James F. *Congregation: Stories and Structures.* Philadelphia: Fortress, 1987.

Lemler, James. *2020: The Vision for Mission Today and Tomorrow.* Cincinnati: Forward Movement Publications, 2003.

Lemler, James, and Charles Fulton. *Truth and Hope.* Cincinnati: Forward Movement Publications, 2006.

————. *Groundwork: Digging Deep for Change and Growth.* New York: Episcopal Church Center, 2005, 2006, 2007. *(There are three separated editions in succession for this evangelism and Lenten spiritual resource.)*

Mann, Alice. *Can Our Church Live? Redeveloping Congregations in Decline.* Herndon, Va.: The Alban Institute, 1999. *(Alice Mann has produced several important and accessible books on congregational development, transitions, and evangelism.)*

McCullough-Bade, Robin and John. *Our Mission: Discovering God's Call to Us.* Minneapolis: Augsburg Fortress, 2002. *(This is one book in the Congregational Leader Series, a very useful set of resources for congregational leadership and development produced by the Evangelical Lutheran Church in America.)*

Mead, Loren. *The Once and Future Church.* Herndon, Va.: The Alban Institute, 1991. *(Loren Mead is one of the great interpreters and teachers regarding congregational life and development. Any of his books are useful.)*

Oswald, Roy M., and Speed B. Leas. *The Inviting Church: A Study of New Member Assimilation.* Herndon, Va.: The Alban Institute, 1987. *(This is a classic text in evangelism and new member ministry.)*

Regele, Mike. *Death of the Church.* Grand Rapids: Zondervan, 1995.

Snow, Luther K. *The Power of Asset Mapping: How Your Congregation Can Act on its Gifts.* Herndon, Va.: The Alban Institute, 2004.

Woods, C. Jeff. *Congregational Megatrends.* Herndon, Va.: The Alban Institute, 1996.

Notes and Sources

notes

1. Cyprian of Carthage, "To Donatus," 4.
2. David Bosch, *Transforming Mission: Paradigm Shifts in Theology of Mission* (Maryknoll, N.Y.: Orbis Books, 1991), 511.
3. "Companions in Transformation," report of the Episcopal Church's Standing Commission on World Mission (2003), 4.
4. Darrell L. Guder, *The Continuing Conversion of the Church: Evangelization as the Heart of Ministry* (Grand Rapids: Eerdmans, 2000), 77–78.
5. Claude Payne and Hamilton Beazley, *Reclaiming the Great Commission: A Practical Model for Transforming Denominations and Congregations* (San Francisco: Jossey-Bass, 2000), 13.
6. The eight Millennium Development Goals are:
   1. Eradicate extreme poverty and hunger.
   2. Achieve universal primary education.
   3. Promote gender equality and empower women.
   4. Reduce child mortality.
   5. Improve maternal health.
   6. Combat HIV/AIDS, malaria and other diseases.
   7. Ensure environmental stability.
   8. Develop a global partnership for development.

These goals reflect the mission of compassion which is at the center of Christian faith and ministry. Though presented by the United Nations, a secular body, they have been embraced by churches throughout the global North as goals for our work of faith in transforming the world.

7. Michael Ramsey, *The Glory of God and the Transfiguration of Christ* (London: Longmans and Green, 1949), 147.

8. Parker Palmer, "Leading from Within," in *Let Your Life Speak* (San Francisco: Jossey-Bass, 2000).

9. Peter Vaill, *Learning as a Way of Being* (San Francisco: Jossey-Bass, 1996), 4, 10–12.

10. William Bridges, *Transitions* (New York: Perseus Books, 1980), 2.

11. Diana Butler Bass, *The Practicing Congregation* (Herndon, Va.: The Alban Institute, 2004), 14.

12. Charles Fulton (Congregational Development Director for the Episcopal Church) and I have written a fuller description of these matters in the monograph *Truth and Hope* (Cincinnati: Forward Movement, 2006).

13. Arlin J. Rothauge, *Sizing Up a Congregation for New Member Ministry* (New York: Episcopal Church Center, 1983).

14. Arlin J. Rothauge, "Congregational Life Cycle" (New York: Episcopal Church Center, 2000). A very useful mode for employing both the congregational size and life cycles frameworks may be found in the Congregational Development Office unit section of the Episcopal Church website: www.episcopalchurch.org

15. Thomas R. Hawkins, *The Learning Congregation* (Louisville: Westminster John Knox Press, 1997), 20–21.

16. Jackson Carroll, from an unpublished paper presented in 2006 for a Lilly Endowment sponsored conference on "Pastoral Excellence."

17. "Toward a Higher Quality of Christian Ministry," a Seabury project, funded by the Lilly Endowment, Inc. (1999). Professor John Dreibelbis, Project Director; Professor David Gortner, Research Director.

18. These areas are modified and expanded from *The Inner Work of Leaders: Leadership as a Habit of Mind* by Barbara Mackoff and Gary Wenet (New York: American Management Association, 2001).

19. Richard Chait, "Follow-Up," *Trustee Leadership Development Manual* (Indianapolis: Trustee Leadership Development, 1997).

20. Robert Wuthnow, *After Heaven: Spirituality in America Since the 1950s* (Berkeley: University of California Press, 1998), 4.

21. Wuthnow, *After Heaven,* 17.

22. Dorothy Bass, ed., *Practicing Our Faith: A Way of Life for a Searching People* (San Francisco: Jossey-Bass, 1998), xi.

23. Craig Dykstra, *Growing in Faith: Education and Christian Practices* (Louisville: Geneva Press, 1999), 3.

24. The Youth Ministry and Spirituality Project, 2005; ymsp.org.

25. Robert Fuller, *Spiritual, But Not Religious* (Oxford: Oxford University Press, 2001), 6.

26. Eddie Gibbs and Ryan Bolger, *Emerging Churches* (Grand Rapids: Baker Publishing Group, 2005), 126.

27. Richard Foster, *Streams of Living Water* (San Francisco: HarperSanFrancisco, 1998), 11–14.

28. John Kotter, *Leading Change* (Cambridge, Mass.: Harvard Business School Press, 1996), 17–18.

---

sources quoted

Quotations set apart within the chapters have been taken from the following books and articles.

Kenda Creasy Dean, Chap Clark, and Dave Rahn, *Starting Right: Thinking Theologically About Youth Ministry* (Grand Rapids: Zondervan, 2001.

Eddie Gibbs and Ryan Bolger, *Emerging Churches* (Grand Rapids: Baker Publishing Group, 2005), 234.

Darrell L. Guder, *The Continuing Conversion of the Church: Evangelization as the Heart of Ministry* (Grand Rapids: Eerdmans, 2000), 77–78.

Parker Palmer, *Let Your Life Speak* (San Francisco: Jossey-Bass, 2000), 85.

Robert Wuthnow, *After Heaven: Spirituality in America Since the 1950s* (Berkeley: University of California Press, 1998), 16.